REDS UNDER THE BED

A graduate in electrical engineering, **Michael Komesaroff** was born in Melbourne, but has spent a large part of his adult life living and working in Asia where he has accumulated a detailed knowledge of the region's mineral industries.

He is also a freelance journalist and has been a frequent contributor to conferences and journals which relate to Asia and its economic development. With a strong interest in public policy, he was Executive in Residence to the School of International Affairs at Pennsylvania State University in 2010 and a member of the advisory board of the Centre for Asian Business at the University of South Australia.

Semi-retired, Komesaroff and his wife recently returned to live in Melbourne where he spends his time writing and lecturing on the wide range of subjects that interest him as well as catching up with old friends and family.

Reds Under the Bed

ASIO and an Unusual Bunch of Suspects

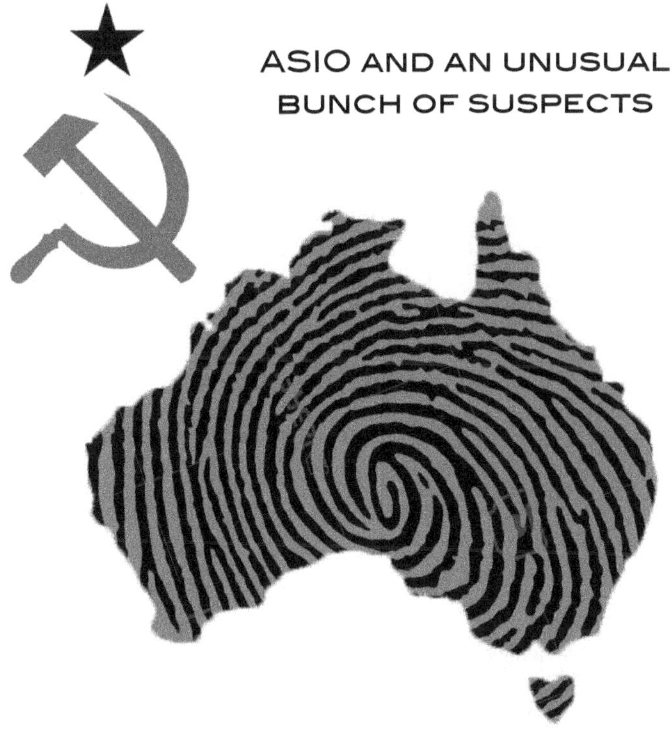

Michael Komesaroff

Hybrid Publishers

Published by Hybrid Publishers

Melbourne Victoria Australia

© Michael Komesaroff 2018

This publication is copyright. Apart from any use
as permitted under the Copyright Act 1968, no part may be
reproduced by any process without prior written permission
from the publisher. Requests and enquiries concerning
reproduction
should be addressed to the Publisher,
Hybrid Publishers,
PO Box 52, Ormond, VIC Australia 3204.
www.hybridpublishers.com.au

First published 2018

ISBN 978-1-925272-98-7

A catalogue record for this book is available from the National Library of Australia

Cover design: Art on Order

As with my other research, this book on the Komesaroff family is dedicated to my grandchildren, Zoe and Asher Komesaroff, and their generational cohorts, so that they will know from where they have come and how privileged they are to live in this wonderful country Australia. It is my hope that one day they will be able to read it and understand that with this privilege comes responsibility.

Contents

Preface and Acknowledgements	ix
Preliminary Notes	xvii
Introduction	1
1 The Komesaroff Family	4
2 ASIO and its Predecessor Organisations	19
3 ASIO's Interest in Jewish Organisations	38
4 The Seven Files on Komesaroff Family Members	64
5 Yaakov Leib Mendelson	74
6 Myer Nathan	94
7 Peter Komesaroff	99
8 Louis Komesaroff	109
9 Max Komesaroff	120
10 Tessa Silberberg	130
11 Morris Komesaroff	136
12 Michael Komesaroff	142

Conclusion	**159**
Appendix	162
Bibliography	165
Endnotes	173

Preface and Acknowledgements

The idea for this book grew out of research about my family's early years in Australia which I undertook in 2014. That research was intended for a publication to commemorate the centennial of the arrival in Australia of my uncle Yaakov Leib Mendelson. I was aware that for most of his time in Australia, Yaakov Leib had been a member of the Communist Party of Australia (CPA), but that he had broken with the Party sometime before his death in 1952. Research of newspaper records revealed little except a letter written by him in 1946 explaining why he had resigned from the Party. This fragment of information encouraged me to understand why my uncle had joined the Party and what occurred that prompted him to leave.

Discussions with people at the National Archives of Australia (NAA) alerted me to the fact that the *Archives Act* 1983 made it possible to access records of the Australian Security Intelligence Organisation (ASIO), the government agency responsible for Australia's domestic security. The NAA librarians guided me through the process and after a few months I was able to access my uncle's ASIO file.

The success with accessing Yaakov Leib's ASIO records encouraged me to apply to read my own file, but unfortunately ASIO reported they did not have one on Michael Benjamin Komesaroff, though they were able to provide a file on a business project based in the Soviet Union that I had worked on in the 1980s. Though disappointed that I did not have an ASIO file, obtaining the organisation's records of my business involvement with the Soviet Union encouraged me to seek further information which culminated in my application to view all the records of first- and second-generation Komesaroff family members. The seven files which were the result of that application form the basis for this book.

I had expected access to ASIO's record would be a lengthy, daunting and frustrating process where the organisation, wanting to protect its secrets, would heavily redact any document they were forced to reveal. My reasoning was that through such obfuscation, the 'spooks' would prevent me from accessing their secrets. I could not have been more wrong. My dealings with ASIO were conducted through the NAA and to my pleasant surprise records were usually provided in an acceptable time frame and on the whole redactions were minimal, though always intriguing. Some of the files were thinner than I had expected which initially led me to believe that they had been 'culled' to remove embarrassing information. However, examination of related files revealed some of the 'missing' information which dispelled my belief in a conspiracy to conceal any uncomfortable evidence. Contrary to my initial expectations, my dealings with NAA and ASIO were efficient and productive, for which I am very grateful.

The provisions of the *Archives Act* 1983 enable citizens to appeal a decision not to release a file or to redact information. In my research I applied for well over 70 files. Some records were not provided because ASIO claimed not to have a relevant file, and many included redactions, usually minor. In all my applications I readily accepted ASIO's decision and at no stage did I contemplate appealing their ruling.

Despite my gratitude to the archivists at NAA and ASIO, I must, however, admit to some residual paranoia arising from occasional hand-written notations within the released files which allude to the existence of additional records that directly relate to the people who were the subjects of my research.

My hope in writing the book is that all the descendants of those Komesaroffs that came to Australia in the first quarter of last century will have a better understanding of our family's history and how our forebears embraced political life in their adopted country.

With the exception of a few who were embarrassed by my research and believe that it should not be discussed outside the immediate family, this work has brought me into closer contact with many of my cousins who kindly shared their memories and heirloom documents with me.

I have used their recollections to supplement the public record, and to these people I am very appreciative. In particular I am thankful to Yaakov Leib's grandson, Roger Mendelson, with whom I have spent many happy hours discussing family history and the political philosophies which guided our ancestors.

Ruth Holan, a daughter of Louis Komesaroff, was an invaluable help with details of her father as well as her sister Tessa Silberberg (née Komesaroff) and brother Max Komesaroff. Ruth's niece, Sue Silberberg, provided details of her mother (Tessa) and offered useful and constructive comments on an early draft of a section of the manuscript. Philip Same and Helen Webberley assisted with details of their grandfather Peter Komesaroff, while Paul Komesaroff and his sister, Illona Komesaroff, helped with information on their father Morris Komesaroff. Because she had divorced and changed her name several times, details of Cecilia Nathan (née Komisaruk) and her children, Myer, Tybel and Moses Nathan, were hard to locate, but I was helped by Motel Zmood, a half-brother to Cecilia's children.

In North America, Edwin Komisaruk and David Usher made time to discuss their experiences growing up in the United States where the family were active in left-wing Jewish politics. Miron Faynerman, formerly of Yerevan in Armenia but now living in New Jersey in the United States, provided details of the descendants of Shlomo Zalman Komisaruk who remained in the Soviet Union. Similarly, in Virginia, but formerly from Minsk in Belarus, Joseph Komissaoruk, Shlomo Zalman's great-grandson, lent me documents which provided details of his grandfather's life under the Soviets.

I owe a great debt to Tom Miller, a long time colleague and friend who for many years edited my contributions to Gavekal Dragonomics Research so that I appear a much more erudite writer than I really am. On this project, Tom gave freely of his time, for which I am eternally grateful. I am also indebted to Anna Fried whose professional skills finessed an earlier version of my research which appeared in the *Journal of the Australian Jewish Historical Society*.[1] As with Tom, Anna's literary skills present me as a more skilful writer than I would otherwise be.

The manuscript has benefited from comments and discussions with Bernard Rechter and Ron Taft. These two nonagenarians, each with an ASIO file, grew up in Melbourne during the 1930s and 40s and knew many of the protagonists referred to in the book, especially the second generation of the Komesaroff family who attended the University of Melbourne.[2]

The book has also benefited greatly from discussions with my oldest friend, Howard Goldenberg. His wisdom and common sense continue to astound me, but not his literary skills nor his friendship and loyalty. My daughter, Deborah Komesaroff, diligently read several drafts of the manuscript and her comments were insightful and constructive. I was also assisted by Ted Plafker, Daniel Plafker, Ron Zmood, Denis Martin and Rod Myer, all of whom were more than generous with their time by reading various versions of the manuscript and offering constructive comments and much appreciated advice. By reading the manuscript these good people saved me from a number of errors of fact and interpretation. Of course, as with any group of people, their opinions diverged so they should not be held accountable for the views expressed in the book. Also, I alone am responsible for any remaining errors.

I want to thank Louis de Vries and Anna Blay of Hybrid Publishers. Without their efforts this would undoubtedly have been a much lesser book. Anna combined efficiency and skill with a careful editorial eye and perceptive questions which contributed greatly to improving the rhetoric, style and quality of my work.

I am indebted to both Adrian Elton and Asher Silvers for their assistance. Adrian used his exceptional skills to edit old family photographs to a standard required for publication while Asher was a tremendous help researching online resources.

My love and thanks to my wife, Sandra Komesaroff, who has always tolerated the many hours I spend in front of my computer or in a library somewhere rather than communicating with her or attending to the tasks she has set me. She continues to support and encourage my eclectic interests, for which I am eternally grateful.

The one regret I have is that none of the group of seven, all of whom were most likely unaware that ASIO was monitoring their activities, are any longer with us, so they remained oblivious of how their lives were invaded by a state that could not distinguish between dissent and subversion. Nothing recorded by ASIO shows any of the seven to be anything other than proud and loyal Australians.

Michael Komesaroff
Malvern, Victoria
May 2018

Preliminary Notes

Names

The Komesaroff family name has varied over time from Komisaruk to Komesarook and Komesaroff. When referring to surnames I use the family name as it was at the time. For example my father William changed his name from Komisaruk (as it was in Russia) to Komesarook (the transliteration of the Cyrillic Komisaruk used by Australian immigration officials) to Komesaroff, the name he adopted around 1933.

Some members of the family changed their name through deed poll or marriage. For example, when he arrived in Australia in 1914, my uncle – Yaakov Leib Mendelson – was known as Yaakov Leib Komesarook, but around 1928 he changed his name to Mendelson by deed poll. On the other hand, Tessa Komesaroff, who was born in Melbourne in 1929, changed her name to Silberberg in 1959 when she married John Silberberg. In this book Tessa is referred to as a Komesaroff until 1959 when she becomes a Silberberg. Similarly, Yaakov Leib is referred to as Yaakov Leib Komesarook until 1928, when he took on the name Mendelson.

In Australia, the Communist Party of Australia (CPA) changed its name to the Australian Communist Party in 1943. In 1951 the Party congress decided to change the name back to the CPA. For simplicity and consistency, I have chosen to refer only to the CPA and not the Australian Communist Party.

Tables

1   Migration details of extended Komesaroff family who migrated to Australia (p. 10)
2   Details of the seven Komesaroff files released by NAA (p. 73)
A1 Descendants of Menachem Mendel Komisaruk (p. 161)
A2 Descendants of Meir Komisaruk (p. 162)

Figures

1   Location of Grafskoy and nearby villages and towns (p. 5)
2   First generation Komesaroff family relationships (p. 7)
3   Menachem Mendel Komisaruk's family at Grafskoy in 1913 (p. 13)
4   Meir Komisaruk's descendants (taken in Ukraine around 1912) (p. 17)
5   Advertisement for Russian publications placed by

Yaakov Leib Mendelson in the Melbourne *Argus*, 6
   June 1945 (p. 78)
6 Yaakov Leib Mendelson (p. 85)
7 Yaakov Leib Mendelson and his family in 1925
   (p. 87)
8 Lionel Hart, Motel Zmood and Myer Nathan (p. 96)
9 Private Peter Komesaroff, No 1684 (p. 105)
10 Louis Komesaroff and his wife Fanny (née Feinberg)
   (p. 115)
11 Louis Komesaroff (p. 117)
12 Max Komesaroff, a graduate in physics and
   optometry from the University of Melbourne (p. 123)
13 Tessa Silberberg (née Komesaroff) and her family
   (p. 132)
14 Morris Komesaroff, a graduate in law from the
   University of Melbourne (p. 135)
15 Joseph Faynerman and his family, Moscow, July
   1986 (p. 146)
16 Michael Komesaroff outside the Kremlin in Red
   Square, Moscow, July 1986 (p. 155)

Abbreviations

AIF	Australian Imperial Force
ALP	Australian Labor Party
ASIB	Australian Special Intelligence Bureau
ASIO	Australian Security Intelligence Organisation
BMR	Bureau of Mineral Resources
CIB	Commonwealth Investigation Branch
CAL	Comalco Aluminium Limited
CIS	Commonwealth Investigation Service

CPA	Communist Party of Australia
CSIRO	Commonwealth Scientific and Industrial Research Organisation
DFAT	Department of Foreign Affairs and Trade
ECAJ	Executive Council of Australian Jewry
IB	Investigation Branch
IWW	Industrial Workers of the World
HMT	Hired Military Transport
JAFC	Jewish anti-Fascist Committee
JCCFA	Jewish Council to Combat Fascism and Anti-Semitism
JWEC	Jewish War Effort Circle
KGB	Soviet Committee for State Security
MGB	Soviet Ministry of State Security
MI5	Military Intelligence Section 5. The security service of the United Kingdom formed in 1909
MJYC	Melbourne Jewish Youth Council
NAA	National Archives of Australia
NSW	New South Wales
NUAUS	National Union of Australian University Students
PRC	People's Republic of China
RMIT	Royal Melbourne Institute of Technology
RSS & AILA	Returned Soldiers', Sailors' and Airmen's Imperial League of Australia
SA	South Australia
USSR	Union of Soviet Socialist Republics
VJBD	Victorian Jewish Board of Deputies
WW I	World War I or the Great War (1914–18)
WWII	World War II (1939–45)

Introduction

For most of the last century, Australia's counter-intelligence organisations monitored the activities of people and organisations it believed were controlled or influenced by the Communist Party of Australia (CPA). As a result of this surveillance, the security services maintained a vast library of files, reputed to cover the details of half a million people, on Australian citizens (as well as residents who were not citizens), the overwhelming majority of whom were never a threat to the country's security.

The fact that Australia's Security Intelligence Organisation (ASIO) raised a file on someone did not necessarily mean they had done anything illegal. As ASIO's official historian David Horne has written:

> At times it seemed that the collection of information became an end in itself. A large amount of anecdotal material was collected and placed on file, with little apparent attempt to reflect on its ramifications or security relevance.[1]

The mammoth collection of files was a consequence of ASIO's objective of excluding CPA members and sympathisers from government or public service positions where they might have access to classified documents. As a result of this objective, ASIO was anxious to establish a comprehensive list of every CPA member which could be used when vetting applicants applying for employment with the government. Indeed, vetting prospective public servants became a major preoccupation for ASIO.[2]

In records released by ASIO I have learnt that the organisation (or its predecessors) kept files on at least seven members of my family. All of the seven were politically active left-of-centre citizens, of whom four were involved with organisations or activities that were either pro-Zionist or opposed to antisemitism. Only two of the seven were ever directly associated with the CPA, though three others were members of groups that were later shown to be controlled by the Communist Party. There is no evidence the three were aware they were members of communist front organisations.

In this book I describe the political lives of the seven people with ASIO files. The book is in four parts. The first part (Chapter 2) provides background to the family relationships and how and when the first generation arrived in Australia. The objective of this section is to describe the family mosaic so readers will understand how individuals relate to each other. Parts two and three (Chapters 3 and 4) provide essential background on the history of Australia's counter-intelligence organisations and the Jewish groups they believed were subversive. These two sections are not intended as definitive histories of Australia's security services nor of the affinity for left-wing causes by some Jews. Instead, they provide essential background explaining why ASIO was created and the reasons the organisation recorded the lives of members of the Komesaroff family. The last part of the book (Chapters 5 to 13) discusses the contents of the seven files and how the information in them was collected. A full biography of the seven people is beyond the scope of this book, which focuses solely on how and why their political activities attracted ASIO's interest.

This four-part structure has been used so that the book does not just document the political activities of the people involved, but also provides a comprehensive understanding and explanation for why Australia's security services took an interest in seven members of my family.

To my surprise and disappointment I could not locate a file on myself, although some of my activities are included in a dossier ASIO created on Comalco Aluminium, a public company I worked for during the 1980s and 1990s. The file – which is mostly made up of telephone intercepts with the Soviet Embassy in Canberra – is discussed in the last part of the book. While it is not a file that reports on me directly, I have included my story because I am probably the only surviving member of my family who can comment on ASIO's record of events from a personal perspective.

1
The Komesaroff Family

The Komesaroff family can trace its history back to early nineteenth century Lithuania, the birthplace of Shlomo Zalman (1798–1853), my great-great-grandfather. At the time of Shlomo Zalman's birth there were no Jewish surnames in Lithuania and people were known by a patronymic. Sometime after his birth and before 1846 when he migrated to Grafskoy, in the Ukraine, Shlomo Zalman was given the surname Komisaruk.[1]

Grafskoy was a Jewish agricultural colony in the Mariupol district of Yekaterinoslav Province in Ukraine, then part of Russia. Grafskoy was renamed Proletarsky by the Soviets and Yekaterinoslav is now known as Dnepropetrovsk, while Ukraine is a sovereign country and no longer part of Russia.

Figure 1 shows the location of Grafskoy and nearby colonies and towns.

Jewish agricultural colonies were established in Russia at the start of the nineteenth century, but Grafskoy was settled somewhat later, around the middle of the century. Shlomo Zalman had come to Grafskoy at the time the colony was settled. The establishment of these agricultural

The Komesaroff Family

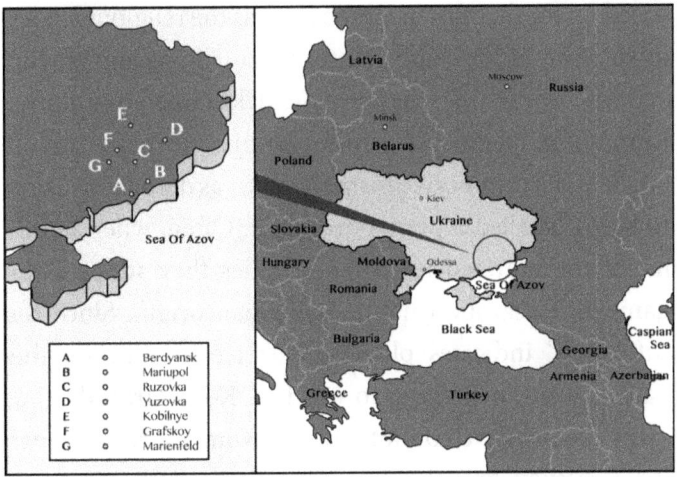

Fig. 1: Location of Grafskoy and nearby colonies and towns

colonies was part of a wider relocation policy formulated by the Russian tsars to settle the rich but sparsely populated agricultural land of southern Russia that had been acquired from the Ottoman Empire, which was then in decline. As incentives, Jews were offered exemption from military service, tax concessions and easy access to land. Special areas, known as Jewish agricultural colonies, were set aside in what was in reality an attempt to reduce the status of Jewish merchants to that of peasants.

In the Yekaterinoslav region of Ukraine there were seventeen Jewish colonies and for administrative purposes each was given a number. Grafskoy was known as colony number seven.

By the time he came to Grafskoy, my great-great-grandfather had been given the surname Komisaruk, based on the fact that as a rabbi he was the religious leader, or *komisar*, of his clan.² The term actually means 'official' and the suffix '*uk*' denotes the Ukrainian diminutive form; so the completed name of Komisaruk means 'minor official'. The diminutive form was seen as derogatory, akin to being labelled a petty bureaucrat. Often, when family members migrated to towns or cities they adopted the name Komesaroff, a name of Russian origin. Since the suffix '*off*' indicates plural possessive in Russian, this name meant 'belonging to officials'. Komesaroff did not carry the negative connotations of Komisaruk. However, the Grafskoy branch of the family used the surname Komisaruk. When they arrived in Australia, immigration officials recorded it as Komesarook, rather than using the more common English transliteration of Komisaruk.³

Shlomo Zalman was the father of four boys, the eldest of whom, Pinkhas (1832–97), also became a rabbi. Pinkhas and his wife Chaya Sara (1834–73) lived in Grafskoy, where they raised seven children – four boys and three girls. Two of the boys, my grandfather Menachem Mendel (1864–1919) and his older brother Meir (1858–1907), are the patriarchs of the two branches of the Komesaroff family that came to Australia in four groups between 1912 and 1922. This was the latter part of the great migration of Jews from Eastern Europe which began in 1881 with the reign of the highly conservative Tsar Alexander III, whose anti-Jewish laws encouraged a series of pogroms which precipitated the largest migration of Jews in modern history. The migration began to

The Komesaroff Family

wane after the Great War when many countries instituted restrictive immigration policies. However, in the latter years of the migration, between 1899 and 1914, around 1.7 million Jews left their *shtetls* for a better life in the New World. The vast majority went to the United States, but many others left for Australia, Canada, Argentina, South Africa and Palestine.

These family relationships are illustrated in Figure 2.

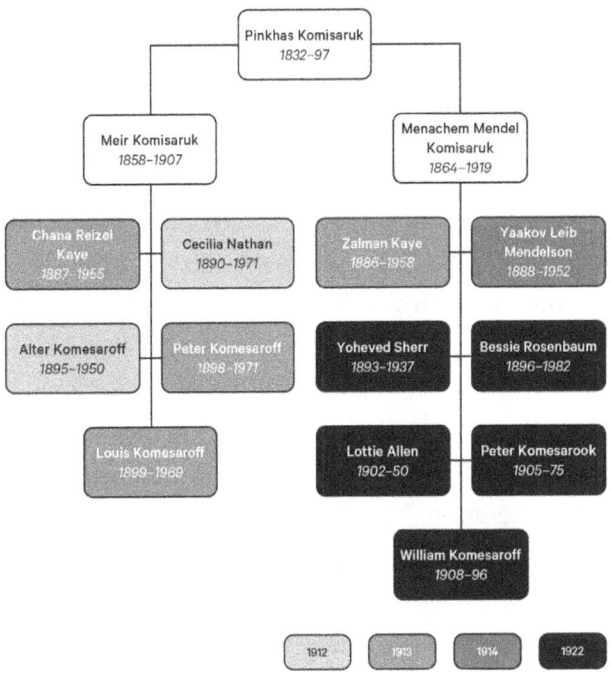

Fig. 2: First generation Komesaroff relationships. The names are those used in Australia. The year in each shaded box below the diagram is the year of arrival in Australia.

In addition to the seven children shown in Figure 2, Menachem Mendel had two other sons, Chaim Zev (1884–1901) and Benjamin (1895–1920), both of whom passed away before the last of their family had left for Australia in 1922.[4] Meir had a young daughter, Chaya Sarah (1906–82), whose mother Tybel (née Zmood, c. 1866–1906) died within days of her birth. Meir himself died the following year and shortly after, Chaya Sarah was adopted by a childless cousin of her mother. When they left Russia, the Australian branch of the family lost contact with Chaya Sarah but in 1923 her brother, Louis Komesaroff, reconnected with her. At that time Chaya Sarah reported that her adopted cousins, with whom she had been living, had died of starvation.[5] During World War II, Chaya Sarah and her family were evacuated to Tashkent in Uzbekistan where she remained for the rest of her life.[6] Apart from Chaya Sarah, none of Menachem Mendel's or Meir's children remained in the Soviet Union.

The twelve people identified in Figure 2 are considered the first generation of migrants to Australia. They were joined by four children who are considered the second generation. The oldest of the sixteen migrants was aged 27 and the youngest, twelve months (see Table 1 for dates of their arrival and other details). Eight of the twelve first-generation migrants married in Australia and raised their children here. Adding in the second generation of descendants born in Australia, this makes a total of 44 Australian people. I am one of those second-generation children, with the last of my generation being born in

1947. A list of the 44 people is provided as Appendix A, which shows that all but thirteen of them have died.

In addition to the four second-generation children, the twelve migrants identified in Figure 2 were accompanied by three family members who are not included in this study because they were not born into the Komesaroff family. My grandmother Beila Reeva Komesaroff (née Pogorelske, 1865–1935), the wife of Menachem Mendel, and Bessie Mendelson (née Svidler, 1894–1974), the wife of Yaakov Leib Mendelson and Esak Sherr (1872–1978), the husband of Yoheved Sherr (née Komisaruk) are not included because they married into the family.

Table 1 on the following page lists all the migrants – not just hereditary family – with the dates and names of the ships they arrived on.

Cecilia Nathan and Alter Komesaroff

The first of the family to migrate to Australia was Meir's daughter Tsiporah (*c.* 1890–1971), who came to Melbourne in 1912 to marry David Zmood (1886–1954), a distant relative of her late mother, Tybel Komisaruk (née Zmood). On the long journey from Russia, Tsiporah was chaperoned by her elder brother Shlomo Zalman (1895–1950). In Australia Tsiporah was known as Cecilia. Her brother, Shlomo Zalman, was known as Alter ('the old one' in Yiddish), as his twin siblings had passed away before he was born, and the custom then among Ashkenazi Jews was to name a succeeding child 'Alter'. Acceptance of the new name was believed to deter the

Table 1: Migration details of extended Komesaroff family who came to Australia

Name*	Date of arrival	Ship	Name recorded on ship's manifest
Cecilia Nathan	10 Oct 1912	SS *Chemnitz*	Tsiporah Comosaroff
Alter Komesaroff	10 Oct 1912	SS *Chemnitz*	Alter Comosaroff
Zalman Kaye	8 Dec 1913	SS *Königin Luise*	Zalman Kommessarook
Chana Reizel Kaye	8 Dec 1913	SS *Königin Luise*	Rese Kommessarook
Tessie Freedman	8 Dec 1913	SS *Königin Luise*	Tube Kommessarook
Myer Kaye	8 Dec 1913	SS *Königin Luise*	Maie Kommessarook
Peter Komesaroff	8 Dec 1913	SS *Königin Luise*	Pinchos Kommessarook
Louis Komesaroff	8 Dec 1913	SS *Königin Luise*	Lebe Kommessarook
Yaakov Leib Mendelson	2 Mar 1914	SS *Friedrich der Grosse*	Jankel Komisaruk
Beila Reeva Komesaroff**	9 Mar 1922	SS *Ballarat*	Beaby Komesarook
Bessie Mendelson**	9 Mar 1922	SS *Ballarat*	Bessie Komesarook
Norman Mendelson	9 Mar 1922	SS *Ballarat*	Norman Komesarook
Esak Sherr**	9 Mar 1922	SS *Ballarat*	Esak Sher
Yoheved Sherr	9 Mar 1922	SS *Ballarat*	Evay Sher
Ben Sherr	9 Mar 1922	SS *Ballarat*	Mendal Sher
Bessie Rosenbaum	9 Mar 1922	SS *Ballarat*	Bessie Komesarook
Lottie Allan	9 Mar 1922	SS *Ballarat*	Zlate Komesarook
Peter Komesarook	9 Mar 1922	SS *Ballarat*	Pnexes Komesarook
William Komesaroff	9 Mar 1922	SS *Ballarat*	Woola Komesarook

Sources: National Archives of Australia, various naturalisation files, Public Record Office Victoria, Index of Unassisted Inward Passenger Lists to Victoria 1852–1923.

*The names are those used in Australia.

**Married into the family; not included in this study.

Angel of Death from visiting the family again.

Cecilia and Alter travelled to Australia on the SS *Chemnitz*, arriving in Melbourne on 10 October 1912.[7] Neither Cecilia nor Alter is known to have files with ASIO, although each of their eldest sons does have an ASIO file. It is likely that there was a file on Cecilia, who had a long-term interest in left-wing politics, but it was probably destroyed after she died and was no longer of interest to ASIO.

Zalman Kaye

The second Komesaroff group to migrate to Australia were Cecilia and Alter's siblings – 28-year-old Chana Reizel (1887–1955), fifteen-year-old Pinkhas (1898–1971) and thirteen-year-old Yehuda Leib (1900–69) – who landed in Melbourne on 8 December 1913 on the SS *Königin Luise*.[8] Chana Reizel was the eldest of Meir Komisaruk's children; when her parents died she took on the responsibility of raising her siblings. When her sister Tsiporah (Cecilia) left Russia, Chana Reizel followed her with her two brothers, Pinkhas (Peter) and Yehuda Leib (Louis). However, by that time she had married and had two children of her own – Tessie (1911–75) and Myer (1909–96). Chana Reizel's husband was her first cousin, Shlomo Zalman Komesarook (1886–1958), the eldest son of Menachem Mendel, a younger brother of her late father Meir. In Australia Shlomo Zalman was known as Zalman, and around 1935 he anglicised his surname to Kaye.

Of the six members of the family who travelled to

Australia in 1913, two – Louis and Peter – have ASIO files, as do two of Louis' children – Max and Tessa.

Yaakov Leib Mendelson

The next Komesaroff to come to Australia was my uncle Yaakov Leib (1888–1952), who arrived aboard the German mail steamer *Friedrich der Grosse*, on 2 March 1914, four months before the outbreak of the Great War (1914–18). Yaakov Leib was Menachem Mendel's second son and the younger brother of Zalman, who had migrated with his family the previous year. While the two earlier groups had migrated to Australia for family reasons, Yaakov Leib's move was motivated by money. He was in dispute with his wife's parents and believed that by coming here he could make sufficient money to return to Russia and repay the dowry they had provided on his marriage to their daughter. Having done that, he reasoned he could live in Russia with his wife and son free of interference from his in-laws. But Yaakov Leib did not return to Russia, for two reasons. One factor was the deterioration of conditions in Russia that accompanied the outbreak of the Great War and the collapse of Russia's Tsarist regime (1917). But the more important reason was the wealth he had accumulated in his short period in Australia. As a result of his hard work – and the generosity and tolerance of Australian society – Yaakov Leib had made more money than he had expected. So it was an easy decision for him to remain here. For my father and the seven other family members who were helped by Yaakov Leib, this

The Komesaroff Family

Fig. 3: Menachem Mendel Komisaruk's family at Grafskoy in 1913. Back row (L to R): Louis Komesaroff (Zelman's brother-in-law and cousin), Zelman Kaye, Yoheved Sherr, Benyomin Komisaruk, Yaakov Leib Mendelson, Bessie Rosenbaum. Middle row: Tessie Freedman, Chana Reizel Kaye, Myer Kaye, Menachem Mendel Komisaruk, William Komesaroff, Beila Reeva Komesaroff, Bessie Mendelson holding Norman Mendelson. Front row: Peter Komesarook, Lottie Allan.

was something for which they were always grateful.

Some years after arriving in Australia, Yaakov Leib became a member of the CPA, so it is understandable that ASIO and its predecessor organisations took an interest in him.

In 1928 Yaakov Leib changed his family name from Komesarook to Mendelson. His father's name was Mendel so his new family name was symbolic: he was the son of Mendel.

Komesaroff, Komesarook, Sherr, Allen and Rosenbaum

The fourth and last group of Komesaroffs to migrate to Australia was Yaakov Leib's immediate family – his widowed mother (my grandmother) Beila Reeva; his wife Bessie; his son (my cousin) Norman (1913–98); his sisters Yoheved (1893–1937), Bessie (1896–1982) and Lottie (1902–50); and his younger brothers Peter (1905–75) and William (my father; 1908–96). The group was joined by Yoheved's husband Esak Sherr and their son, my cousin Ben Sherr (1921–2009). The group travelled to Australia on the SS *Ballarat*, landing in Adelaide on 9 March 1922 before moving on to Melbourne by train. The group arrived in Melbourne in March 1922, a decade before the large scale migration of non-English-speaking Jews which was to transform Jewish life in Australia.

Unlike the three previous groups that had come to Australia, this last and largest group encountered strong administrative resistance to their migration. Their difficulties were mostly a consequence of the Bolshevik Revolution, which increased Australia's fear of communism and foreigners.[9] Government policy after the Great War was opposed to migration from Russia, because it regarded the chaos that plagued Australian industry after the War as incited by foreign Bolshevik agitators.[10] There was also a fear that communist sympathisers could attempt a similar revolution in Australia. Not only did these fears impact immigration from Russia, but they also shaped the policies of Australia's embryonic security services, which until recent times devoted the bulk of their resources to the detection and surveillance of communists and their sympathisers.

Concern about Soviet influence in Australia was heightened in March 1919, following widespread social unrest in Brisbane, where communist-led unionists who were protesting against continuation of the *War Precautions Act*, clashed with recently returned soldiers.[11] The protesters carried red flags, a symbol of socialism which was banned under the *Act*, and the protests became known as the 'Red Flag' riots. Mistrust of the communists and the anti-war movement had increased after the March 1918 signing of the Treaty of Brest-Litovsk, when Russia's post-revolutionary communist government sued for peace with Germany after previously fighting alongside Britain and its allies, including Australia. In the public mind this linked Germany and Russia together as a common foe.[12]

Yaakov Leib, now a successful businessman, lobbied tirelessly to obtain an exemption from the government's restriction on Russian migration so that his family could come to Australia. He petitioned federal politicians and a number of other public figures, mostly supporters of the Labor Party and people with social and political beliefs that aligned with his own. The lobbying was effective, and in February 1921 Federal Cabinet gave approval for Yaakov Leib's family to enter Australia.

The other Komesaroffs

Pinkhas Komisaruk's other children and their descendants migrated to Canada and the United States, though a few remained in what was to become the Soviet Union. One of those who remained in the Soviet Union was Pinkhas' eldest son, Shlomo Zalman (1855–1920), an older brother to my grandfather Menachem Mendel. One of Shlomo Zalman's sons, Motel or Mark Komisaruk (1887–1970) wrote an extensive diary which is now in the possession of one of his grandsons, Joseph Komissarouk (1947–), who migrated to the United States in 1992. The diary is written in Yiddish and records the life of a pious Jew who, despite the communist government's attitude to religious observance and Jewish observance in particular, continued to attend regular synagogue services until late in his life. Others who knew Mark describe him as a learned man who, during Soviet times, was consulted by his coreligionists who were no longer able to learn the reasons for the religious practices that they had performed as young children in pre-revolutionary Russia.

Preliminary research on the North American side of the family suggest they were, like their Australian cousins, ardent Zionists, though they tended to be more secular in their Jewish observance. A number were members of socialist organisations, including the fraternal order Jewish Workmen's Circle, the secular Jewish socialist group The Bund and the Marxist Poale Zion (Workers of Zion).[13] While all their second-generation male cousins in Australia celebrated their bar mitzvah, this was not the

The Komesaroff Family

Fig. 4: Meir Komisaruk's descendants (taken in Ukraine around 1912). Back row (L to R): Louis Komesaroff, Cecilia Nathan, 'Alter' Komesaroff, Tessie Freedman. Front row: Peter Komesaroff, Zalman Kaye, Myer Kaye, Chana Reizel Kaye.

case in the United States where many in the family did not attend synagogue regularly. In North America the family's political allegiance was typical of other Jewish immigrants from Eastern Europe who formed a substantial core of early twentieth century progressives and socialists.[14]

Leon Komisaruk of Detroit typifies Pinkhas Komisaruk's descendants who settled in America. Though a secular Jew and an anti-communist, he held very liberal views and was a fervent Zionist who was a regular and generous benefactor to Jewish causes. Leon was instrumental in rescuing members of his family from Russia when it was imploding under the turmoil of civil war. He later changed his surname from Komisaruk to Kaye.

2
ASIO and its Predecessor Organisations

The history of ASIO is well documented, its creation being a response to the United States and Britain suspending their intelligence collaboration with Australia. Many Australians may be aware that a US counter-intelligence program to decrypt secret messages transmitted by Soviet intelligence agencies – the Venona project, which ran from 1943 to 1980 – confirmed that the Soviets had penetrated Australian government departments shortly after diplomatic relations between the Soviet Union and Australia were initiated in 1943.

The Department of External Affairs (later the Department of Foreign Affairs, now the Department of Foreign Affairs and Trade) had been severely compromised by a spy ring controlled by a CPA functionary, Wally Clayton. Clayton died in 1997, but did not admit to his activities until very late in his life; yet the counter-espionage authorities were able to confirm that for several years he had passed state secrets to his Soviet handler, Feodor Nosov, the correspondent in Australia for TASS, the Soviet newsagency.[1] In 1993 a former National Secretary of the CPA, Laurie Aarons, surreptitiously recorded an interview with Clayton in which the spymaster not only admitted to his espionage but also confirmed that it had been approved by senior CPA officials.[2]

A life-long communist, Clayton was said to have been embarrassed when he was paid for documents he provided, because, as he explained to his Soviet handler, he had passed information as a 'duty'.[3] Similarly, most of Clayton's informants were either members of the Party or close acquaintances of communists who were aware that the information they provided was destined for Moscow.[4]

The clandestine activities of Clayton and his cohorts represented a fifth column in the Department of External Affairs, and in 1946 a Canadian Royal Commission on Espionage similarly concluded that a fifth column organised by Soviet diplomats existed in Canada and that the communist movement was the principal base from which the espionage network was recruited. In its report the Commission was appalled at how Soviet agents were able to find Canadians who were willing to betray their country and to supply agents of a foreign power secret information to which they had access, despite oaths of allegiance, of office and of secrecy which they had taken.[5]

The same could be said about Wally Clayton and his CPA cohorts who betrayed Australia by providing the Soviet Union with state secrets that many of them had sworn to protect.

The Soviet intercepts provided by the Venona

project, some of which began to be released by the US National Security Agency in 1995, reveal that, because of Australia's close alliance with Britain and the US, Moscow had obtained highly classified intelligence through their Australian agents. Our allies reacted to the theft of their secrets by suspending intelligence collaboration with Australia and pressuring the government to create a security organisation modelled on MI5, Britain's domestic counter-intelligence and security agency, although there were Australian predecessors to the new agency, which are described later in this chapter.

The new agency, the Australian Security Intelligence Organisation (ASIO) – Australia's first truly nationwide counter-intelligence organisation – was created on 16 March 1949, not by any decision of parliament, but by a ten-point administrative fiat issued by the then Prime Minister, Ben Chifley. Titled 'Memorandum to the Director-General of Security, being a directive for the establishment and maintenance of a security service', the decree included the appointment of Geoffrey Reed, Justice of the Supreme Court of South Australia, as the Director-General of Security.[6] Chifley's directive did not provide for any judicial or administrative oversight of the new service.

Reed had been seconded from South Australia for twelve months, and the appointment of a member of the judiciary to lead the new intelligence organisation reflected Chifley's desire that the new service should undertake its work impartially and not favour any particular political group. With the dawning of the Cold War the Labor Government probably feared a security service that would target the leftist section of the political spectrum. Labor's concerns can be seen in point six of the ten-point memorandum that gave rise to ASIO:

> It is essential that the Security Service should be kept absolutely free from any political bias or influence, and nothing should be done that might lend colour to any suggestion that it is concerned with the interests of any particular section of the community, or with any matters other than the defence of the Commonwealth. You will impress on your staff that they have no connection whatever with any matters of a party political character and they must be scrupulous to avoid any action which could be so construed.[7]

Reed's appointment by Chifley, a Labor Prime Minister, was somewhat unusual. While Reed had some experience with security matters as chairman of a state committee that dealt with objections to war-time internment of foreign nationals, he was known to be a 'stout individualist' with a particular dislike for Labor politicians.[8]

In their book *Breaking the Codes*, Desmond Ball and David Horner explain that the Department of External Affairs was so severely compromised by Clayton and his team that the first fifteen months of ASIO's existence were devoted to investigating the penetration of the Department by communist agents.[9] Because of the circumstances under which it was created, and despite the prohibition in its initial mandate, ASIO's earliest activities were directed against left-leaning organisations, especially those, such as the CPA, that were seen to be controlled by the Soviet Union.

However, Australia's fear of communism predated the creation of ASIO, as can be seen by the government's reaction to the 'Red Flag' riots of 1919. Some of the 'Red Flag' protest leaders were Russian-born communists who were sent to Australia as representatives of the post-revolutionary Bolshevik government – clear evidence that Soviet interest in Australia existed well before ASIO was established. The Australian government's attitude to the riots and the Bolshevik perpetrators is summed up in a memo written by William Watt (acting Prime Minister from April 1918 to August 1919) who described the protesters 'as distinctly undesirable Russian Bolsheviks'. With the collapse of Tsarism many of these Russians were anxious to return to their country of birth and Watt urged 'that the Government should place no obstacle in the way of their returning to Russia'.[10]

In the years immediately after federation (1901), Australia had seen no need for a counter-intelligence organisation, but that had changed with the Great War, when the Secretary of State for the Colonies (Andrew Bonar Law) directed a secret memorandum to the Governor General (Sir Ronald Munro-Ferguson) suggesting that Australia create a branch of the Imperial Counter Espionage Bureau. This branch, known as the Australian

Special Intelligence Bureau (ASIB), was established in January 1916 and maintained a close relationship with state police forces, and later with the Commonwealth Police Force. As with the creation of ASIO many years later, the ASIB was not the product of parliamentary legislation but was the result of an administrative decision made by the government. Also, as with ASIO's early years, the ASIB was not the subject of parliamentary oversight, which made it easy for the government to use the Bureau to monitor its political opponents.

In 1919, the Commonwealth Police Force and the ASIB merged to form the Investigation Branch (IB) within the Commonwealth Attorney General's Department. The IB, later known as the Commonwealth Investigation Branch (CIB) and later again as the Commonwealth Investigation Service (CIS), was a relatively small organisation that depended on assistance from state police, especially when the provisions of the *War Precautions Act* were applied.[11] The state police also helped their federal colleagues to register foreign residents and to investigate people applying for an Australian visa as well as for immigrants applying for naturalisation.

From its inception, the ASIB – and later the IB and the CIS – concentrated on anti-war and anarchist groups such as the Marxist-inspired Industrial Workers of the World (IWW), which, in 1916, the government had declared an illegal organisation. Supporters of *Sinn Fein*, a political group that sought independence for Ireland and was opposed to the Great War, were also monitored.

Later, after the 1917 Russian Revolution, attention was directed to the threat from communism.[12] A similar situation existed in the United States where militant IWW affiliates mailed explosives to prominent members of America's economic and political establishment, exacerbating community tensions and culminating in the first of the so-called 'Red Scares'.[13]

That many governments, including the Australian government, were concerned with the threat from communism owed much to the fact that when the communists overthrew the Romanov rulers of Russia, they repudiated all of Russia's national debt and expropriated, without compensation, all foreign interests in the country. Such acts, together with the claim by Lenin that he was committed to world revolution, made Russia a global pariah and led foreign governments to take the communist threat very seriously.

The IB initiated its surveillance of communist organisations in the wake of the 1919 'Red Flag' riots, and this surveillance was reinforced with the formation, in 1920, of the CPA, which was endorsed by the Comintern in 1923. The Comintern, also known as the Third International and the Communist International, was formed in 1919 by Russia's Communist Party, and was intended to be the world party of revolution. Essentially, any political party anywhere in the world that wished to be known as 'communist' required the Comintern's authorisation. In return for this recognition, the different communist parties were required to support all the decisions made by the Comintern's Moscow executive, including who should lead the party and what policies it should pursue. Effectively, the communist leadership in Russia had absolute power over the foreign constituent organisations.[14]

In addition to the requirement for strict discipline, Party members were expected to make extraordinary sacrifices, including the suppression of all personal feelings and loyalties, so that they would be prepared to advance the interests of the Party ahead of the interests of family and friends.[15] In Australia, as in other countries, the local Party branch slavishly followed the dictates emanating from Moscow where the Comintern brooked no criticism. Until 1943, when the Comintern was dissolved and its work transferred to the International Department of the Central Committee of the Communist Party of the Soviet Union, Australian members of the CPA were billed a small annual fee of two shillings which was designated as an 'international levy' and was somehow linked to the Comintern.

During the 1930s and 1940s the CPA sent representatives to Moscow to attend Comintern conferences and report on the prospects for revolution in Australia, while the Comintern periodically dispatched representatives to Australia where they approved key CPA office-holders and confirmed that the Comintern's orders were being followed.[16] Adherence to Moscow's line was further reinforced by local members who attended the International Lenin School in Moscow for lengthy periods of study that were designed to train disciplined and reliable political cadres. David Lowell, who has written widely on the CPA's association with the Comintern, observes that party members seem to have been remarkably compliant with changes in the 'line' coming from Moscow; even the about-face in Soviet policy towards Nazi Germany – signalled by the 1939 Molotov-Ribbentrop pact, after which the Soviets redefined World War II as an Imperialistic War instead of a War of Fascist Aggression – did not lead to large numbers leaving the Party.[17] This, despite the fact that in the year preceding the Pact, CPA publications had regularly lambasted Hitler, describing him as 'a barbarous monster' and 'a deadly threat to peace' who should be resisted. Before the Pact's announcement, communists in the West denied that a treaty with Germany would be signed, denouncing such rumours as 'fascist propaganda'.[18]

Earlier, in 1929, another decision of the Comintern tested the loyalty of Jews who supported communism, especially those who were also Zionists and wanted to transform the British mandate in Palestine to a Jewish homeland. On 15 August, more than 1,000 Arabs rioted in Hebron, resulting in the death of 69 Jews. The Grand Mufti of Jerusalem, Haj Amin al Husseini, the speaker in the mosque that day, had incited Arab worshippers to violence. In the United States, *Morgen Freiheit*, the communist-affiliated Yiddish-language daily newspaper, initially described the riots as a pogrom, but quickly fell into line with Moscow's interpretation of events, calling the riots an Arab uprising against British and

Zionist imperialists which had been provoked by 'Zionist-Fascists'.[19] The predominantly Jewish Palestine Communist Party also followed the Kremlin's directive and glorified the 'national revolutionary nature' of the anti-Jewish riots. As a result of this incident some Jewish members became disillusioned and deserted the Party, but most continued as devoted adherents of communist ideology.

In Australia, my uncle Yaakov Leib Mendelson, the only Komesaroff confirmed to be a CPA member, remained with the Party throughout World War II and only resigned in 1946 because he disagreed with Soviet policies toward the creation of a Jewish state. Throughout the War, another Komesaroff, Myer Nathan, son of Cecilia Nathan (née Komisaruk and cousin to Yaakov Leib), who was believed to have been a member of the CPA, continued to spout the Party's line that the Soviet Union's 1939 marriage of convenience with Nazi Germany (the Molotov-Ribbentrop pact) was forced upon Stalin when Britain and France refused to form a military alliance with the Soviet Union that would have contained Hitler.[20] The academic Philip Mendes argues that the fact that my uncle and other communists of Jewish origin chose to remain in the Party despite the Soviet alliance with Hitler suggests their Party affiliation was far more important than their national identity as Jews.[21] I would not confine this observation to Party members who were Jewish but would expand it to include all CPA members. At the outbreak of the War, Moscow directed its Australian followers to frustrate the national war effort by not enlisting in the armed services and by urging trade-unionists to boycott the export of war materials. In complying with this directive from a foreign country that was aligned with Australia's enemy, Australia's communists were demonstrating that their Party affiliation was far more important than their Australian identity or loyalty.

The two issues that almost certainly raised the concerns of security agencies in Australia and other non-communist countries were the funding that the Comintern provided to its national affiliates and the requirement that affiliates establish a parallel, but underground, organisation that could pursue Moscow's policies if the local Party was declared illegal. There is ample evidence to show that, from its inception, the Comintern made substantial payments to support local communist parties and that, without the Soviet funding, the CPA could not have functioned. Documents compiled by the Comintern's first representative in Australia, Aleksander Zuzenko, confirm that Moscow was prepared to make extensive payments so that member parties could push the communist line in their home countries. In the 1930s, Australia's Military Intelligence believed the CPA was receiving at least £500 per year from Moscow.[22] In addition to organisational allocations, the Comintern also made significant payments to individual operatives, for example, S. Mason, the CPA's representative to the Comintern in 1936, wrote asking for a grant of £5,000 as his fare to Russia had consumed most of his money.[23] In

1952 when Lance Sharkey, the CPA's Secretary-General visited Moscow to attend the Nineteenth Congress of the Communist Party of the Soviet Union, the Soviets agreed to provide him with US$25,000 to sustain the operations of its Australian franchise.[24] In his history of the CPA, the former member Stuart Macintyre recounts how, during the 1930s, members returning from the Soviet Union would carry wads of cash to supplement the Party's coffers.[25] ASIO's records reveal that Moscow continued to bankroll its Australian supplicants until at least 1967.[26]

Moscow's exhortation to its affiliates that they establish parallel, and possibly illegal, organisations is contained in the *Conditions of Admission to the Communist International*, a document which details 21 non-negotiable prerequisites that were to be satisfied by a national Communist Party wishing to affiliate with the Comintern. The third condition states:

> In almost every country in Europe and America the class struggle is entering the phase of civil war. Under such conditions the communists can place no trust in bourgeois legality. They have the obligation of setting up a parallel organisational apparatus which, at the decisive moment, can assist the party to do its duty to the revolution. In every country where a state of siege or emergency laws deprive the communists of the opportunity of carrying on all their work legally, it is absolutely necessary to combine legal and illegal activity.[27]

Clandestine activities such as illicit funding, the creation of underground Party cells and other similar illegal activities, including the printing of forged passports and the managing of 'safe houses', were the responsibility of the Comintern's international liaison service.[28] This is the same Comintern to which non-Soviet Pact members, including those in Australia, pledged their allegiance and gave their fealty.

Comintern funding, demands for total obedience to Moscow's policies and the creation of illegal underground cells combined to create an environment where CPA members, like Wally Clayton, believed it was their duty to betray their country by passing state secrets to their Soviet controllers. This was an environment that changed people: it was said that the prominent Australian author and life-long communist, Katharine Susannah Pritchard, transformed from a kind and gentle mother to a ruthless apparatchik willing to do anything to advance the Soviet cause.[29] In Britain, another communist author, Doris Lessing, abandoned a husband and two children to devote herself to communism and creating a free world in which her estranged children could grow up.[30] For Pritchard and Lessing, as well as countless other Party faithful, communism was a life of total commitment. In such an environment CPA members were a legitimate intelligence target and any counter-espionage agency would have inevitably monitored the Party's activities. While this personal view is an unambiguous and unreserved endorsement of ASIO's anti-communist objectives, it would be a mistake to extend my assessment to support for the intrusive and partisan tactics that the organisation used to pursue its mission.

Some people, especially those on the extreme left of the political spectrum, who do not appreciate that the prime function of the state is to protect its citizens, would disband organisations like ASIO rather than grapple with critical philosophical issues such as the balance of power between individuals and the state: the balance between national security that is necessary to safeguard the community and the equally important need to protect that community's civil rights. Such philosophical issues were also canvassed by Justice Robert Hope of the NSW Supreme Court who in 1974 was appointed a Royal Commissioner to conduct an enquiry into Australia's intelligence agencies.[31] Prior to 1969, when he was appointed a judge, Hope had been active in the field of civil liberties and for a period (1967–69) had been president of the Council of Civil Liberties. With Justice Hope's strong libertarian background, ASIO's critics expected that his reports would be very critical of the organisation and possibly recommend that it be disbanded. This expectation was reinforced because Hope's appointment as a Royal Commissioner had been recommended by a Labor Prime Minister – Gough Whitlam. However, Hope's performance as a Royal Commissioner demonstrated that he understood the need to balance state power with human rights. He acknowledged that a security agency was essential for Australia's national interest and his recommendations were aimed at increasing ASIO's accountability while concurrently enhancing its effectiveness. I return to Justice Hope's enquiry later in this chapter.

Geoffrey Reed's secondment to ASIO ended in July 1950 when he stood down as the organisation's Director-General and returned to the South Australian Supreme Court. He was replaced by Colonel (later Brigadier Sir) Charles Spry, a Duntroon graduate who, at the time of his appointment to ASIO, was Australia's Director of Military Intelligence. Spry was to head ASIO for 20 years and under his leadership ASIO emerged as an ideologically-driven organisation that was run along military lines as his personal fiefdom.[32] The organisation's culture was anything but impartial, and throughout Spry's tenure the Labor Party regularly criticised him for favouring their conservative opponents. W. C. Wentworth, a resolutely anti-communist parliamentarian, requested and received personal briefings on political enemies. The organisation also provided a detailed briefing on the radical student movement for the Liberal Party while ministers of the Federal Liberal government sought and received ASIO assistance to research aspects of the personal lives of their Labor opponents.[33] Under Spry's leadership, ASIO research papers were regularly sent to right-wing journalists and anti-communist organisations.[34]

Spry's partisan political alliance with the conservative government had a corrosive effect within his organisation, as ASIO's officers came to believe that leftist dissent indicated disloyalty. Supporters of public policy positions on issues that were at odds with the government's policy, such as feminism, social welfare and the plight of indigenous Australians, were seen by the ASIO agents as likely traitors. Today these issues are viewed as relatively mainstream.[35]

Evidence of ASIO's partisan and unprofessional use of intelligence material was cited by the Hope Royal Commission, established by Gough Whitlam in 1974 to examine Australia's intelligence agencies. This Royal Commission was the first independent assessment of national security since the formation of ASIO in 1949. In the Commission's report issued in 1977, Justice Hope observed that ASIO needed to have the confidence of all political parties, and that if it became directly involved in the public dissemination of security intelligence, it could rightfully be accused of taking a partisan political position that would harm its reputation.[36]

Justice Hope also censured ASIO for not paying more attention to assessing the reliability of its intelligence sources, their credibility and the relevance of the information they supplied. He was also critical of the organisation's culture, which did not see analysis and assessment as its central role, and he quoted serving officers who described some of their colleagues as 'great clippers of newspapers' and 'not people with an inclination to delve into the meaning of things'.[37] Another officer recalled: 'I never had one hour of discussion intellectually about what the organisation was doing'.[38] A former communist himself and the subject of an extensive ASIO file, David McKnight has described the organisation's files as 'a repository for bits and pieces' rather than 'a considered assessment'.[39] These views are supported by David Horner, ASIO's official historian, who observed that at times it seemed the collection of information became an end in itself. A large amount of anecdotal material was placed on file, with little apparent attempt to reflect on its ramifications or security relevance.[40] The consistent theme of these comments that data collection and not analysis was the objective is confirmed by the seven Komesaroff files which contain a jumble of data, much of it irrelevant, inaccurate and uncorroborated.

In 1983, six years after the Royal Commission Report, Justice Hope led a second far-reaching Royal Commission, which again examined aspects of Australia's security and intelligence agencies. On this occasion he found that many of his earlier recommendations had been implemented, but he also observed that ASIO's filing system still left a lot to be desired:

> Too often files appear to be repositories in which information is placed without much (or sometimes any) thought. There is little sign of effort to review files on a regular basis, or to analyse, distil and reduce the contents. A lot of files I have seen are larger than they need to be and reflect little considered review and assessment of the information that they hold.[41]

The monitoring of a large number of 'front'

organisations also contributed to ASIO's files being particularly voluminous. A communist 'front' organisation was defined as a body that operated under communist direction but with no overt sign of control by either the party or the Soviet Union. Many of the Jewish groups covered in this book bear the hallmarks of classic 'front' organisations. For example, the Jewish Council to Combat Fascism and Anti-Semitism (JCCFA) was modelled on a similar Soviet group that Moscow had established in the dark days of World War II as a means of eliciting western support for its war effort. Many of the early members of the JCCFA in Australia were also supporters of the CPA, but apart from the executive secretary, none of the initial executive committee, which included Peter Komesaroff, was associated with the Party, although they were all passionate supporters of the Council's stated aims of defeating fascism and combating antisemitism.

In the years immediately after World War II, the Labor Club at the University of Melbourne was another 'front' organisation with communists constituting the decisive force that shaped its policy. Prior to Labor Club meetings, the local university Party branch discussed the Club's agenda and when this was agreed on, CPA members proposed the items as Club policy. Non-Party members, which included members of the Komesaroff clan, were unaware that the communists had caucused prior to the Club's meeting. The Labor Club was also used by the CPA to 'talent spot' and recruit new members.[42]

A note circulated in 1940 to Queensland members of

the Party suggests that the CPA believed that the Council for Civil Liberties, another group that was supported by the Komesaroff tribe, was a front organisation. At a time the Party was illegal and members were advised to call the Council if they were detained by the police because 'any action taken by the Council for Civil Liberties, of course, is determined wholly by the Party'.[43]

In the next chapter I discuss Australian front organisations that the communists set up with the intention of attracting support from both secular and observant Jews.

3
ASIO's Interest in Jewish Organisations

In addition to maintaining files on individuals they suspected of being subversive foreign agents, ASIO and its predecessors kept close watch on organisations they believed wanted to do harm to Australia. Usually it was membership of such organisations that brought people to ASIO's attention and this was certainly the case with the seven members of my family who are known to have ASIO files. For example, my father's first cousins, the brothers Peter and Louis Komesaroff, were prominent in the activities of the Jewish Council to Combat Fascism and Anti-Semitism (JCCFA) – which ASIO considered a communist 'front' organisation. As a result the two brothers (and others associated with the Council) were put on a watch list. Similarly, Louis' elder daughter, Tessa Silberberg (née Komesaroff), who was a politically active though moderate social democrat, has an ASIO file; her name was found on a subscription list for the Australasian Book Society, an organisation described by ASIO as a publisher 'of selected books in cheap editions' and a distributor of 'books of a leftish nature'.[1] Because ASIO believed the Society was a 'propaganda agency fostered (if not fathered) by the CPA', people who were associated with it were placed under varying degrees of surveillance.[2] Targeting someone for no other reason than they subscribed to a magazine suggests that ASIO did not distinguish between dissent and subversion. A similar view was expressed by Justice Hope in a report of the first of two Royal Commissions on Intelligence and Security, in which he concluded that 'ASIO officers have shown a tendency to think of anyone they chose to call "left-wing" as subversive'.[3]

ASIO's interest in Jewish organisations began shortly after its creation when it appointed a field officer to monitor subversive activities among aliens and the Jewish community. In addition to monitoring the Jewish fraction of the CPA, ASIO also monitored front groups that the communists had promoted as a means of appealing to both secular and religious Jews.[4] The idea of working through front organisations was articulated by Lenin in his 1902 manifesto, *What Is To Be Done?* At that time communism was illegal in Russia, so Lenin proposed reaching the masses through other organisations with a much wider membership.[5] Created and controlled by the Party, front groups attracted people of goodwill who unwittingly gave legitimacy to the communists' activities. The primary purpose of a front was to extend communist influence into areas where an openly communist appeal would not receive support, a task the Party sought to accomplish by concealing their real objectives behind a morally appealing reform such as combating fascism and antisemitism.[6] In his history of the CPA, Stuart Macintyre claims that in the 1930s the Australian Communist Party established fruitful connections to Jewish cultural bodies and community organisations, and ASIO files show that this practice continued in the 1940s, when Jewish CPA members were directed to establish links with Jewish communal organisations.[7]

Of all the Jewish organisations monitored by ASIO or its predecessors, none seemed to have received more attention than the JCCFA. The Council was created in Melbourne in May 1942 by a group of predominantly Eastern European Jews with strong Jewish national and cultural loyalties who were long-established in Australia.[8] As with other groups that were under communist influence, the JCCFA appears to have been modelled on a similar Soviet organisation, the Jewish anti-Fascist Committee (JAFC), which the Soviets had created a few months earlier (February 1942). Moscow's intention was that the JAFC would promote a pro-Soviet public opinion among Jews in foreign countries so they would be encouraged to support the Soviet war effort.[9] The JAFC was dissolved in 1948 on Stalin's orders; its leaders were detained and some were murdered. The JAFC's fate was a consequence of Moscow's concern that, with the end of the War, the Committee no longer served a purpose and its activities were becoming too Zionistic. This contributed to strengthening the 'Jewish reactionary bourgeois-nationalist movement abroad' and 'nationalist, Zionist sentiment among the Jewish population of the USSR'.[10]

To justify the closure of the JAFC, the Soviet Ministry of State Security (MGB) accused the Committee's leadership of involvement in an American Zionist plot that was hatched when they travelled to the United States to raise funds and support for the Soviet war-effort. The MGB alleged that while in America the leadership had conspired with 'American capitalist interests' to create a 'Jewish state in Crimea'.[11] The arrests that followed the campaign to discredit the JAFC paved the way for the infamous, but non-existent, 'Doctors' Plot' and other state-sponsored antisemitic atrocities that decimated the USSR's Jewish intellectual elite and repressed any manifestation of Zionism and Jewish culture. As a result of such Soviet actions, some Jews left the CPA because they had become disillusioned with communism.

In Australia the JCCFA's early leadership included Jewish left-leaning social democrats like the Komesaroff brothers (Peter and Louis), as well as Jewish members of the CPA like my uncle, Yaakov Leib Mendelson.[12] As indicated by its name, the Council was concerned with the threat from antisemitism, both locally and internationally, which its members linked to the rise of fascism in Europe. They also saw antisemitism in Australia as a product of the conservative side of politics, exemplified by the actions of right-wing politicians such as Henry Gullett, who campaigned against the immigration of

Jewish refugees fleeing Nazi-occupied Europe, as did the authors of articles in sensationalist tabloid publications such as the Melbourne *Truth* and *Smith's Weekly*.[13]

Gullett, a conservative member of the House of Representatives, was a notorious Jew-baiter, who used his presence in the federal parliament to attack Jews who had escaped the Holocaust by migrating to Australia, describing them as 'exploiters of labour' who had 'evaded income tax'.[14] Later, in a letter to the Melbourne *Argus* in February 1947, Gullett railed against the admission of Holocaust survivors to Australia, which he described as 'a national tragedy', as he alleged they could not be successfully absorbed into the community 'because they owe loyalty and allegiance to no one'. He also alleged it was such behaviour that precipitated Hitler's Final Solution.[15] In 1969 the political scientist Peter Medding described Gullett's letter as 'probably the most vicious Anti-semitic attack ever made in Australia by a person in public life'.[16]

The failure of Gullett's conservative colleagues to censure him provoked a storm of protest from his political opponents on the left, with some pointing out that the politician's words bore a close similarity to those of Hitler's *Mein Kampf* and the violently antisemitic Nazi journal *Der Stürmer*.[17] And Gullett's sentiments were not unique among his conservative colleagues. For example, Rupert Ryan, the United Australia Party member for the Victorian electorate of Flinders, announced to the House of Representatives in 1945 that he did not mind admitting Polish Jews to Australia, but he thought non-Jewish Poles would make better Australian citizens.[18]

The criticism from the left, linked with the silence of Gullett's party colleagues, enhanced Jewish support for non-conservative politicians. The fact that the left were strong supporters of the creation of the State of Israel, the Australian Labor Party (ALP) in particular, helped to accentuate this difference. Indeed, Dr H. V. Evatt, the ALP deputy Prime Minister and Minister for External Affairs (later leader of his party) is generally acknowledged to have been the midwife at the birth of the Jewish state. Evatt is credited with drafting the partition resolution – voted on in 1947 – that secured Israel's independence.[19] As the respected historian Bill Rubinstein notes, Australian Jews reciprocated the friendliness of the ALP with their loyal support: at the time, and for many years afterwards, the vast majority of Australia's Jewish citizens gave their electoral support to the Labor Party.[20]

Until shortly after World War II, global communism was generally seen to be sympathetic to Jews and to the idea of a Jewish state with Lenin having acknowledged Jews as a legitimate nationality. In his *Critical Remarks on the National Question*, which he wrote around 1913, Lenin stated:

> ... it is beyond doubt that in order to eliminate all national oppression it is very important to create autonomous areas, however small, with entirely homogeneous populations, towards which members of the respective nationalities scattered all over the country, or even all over

the world, could gravitate, and with which they could enter into relations and free associations of every kind.[21]

While this passage does not specifically refer to Jews, it does demonstrate that certainly in his early years Lenin did not see any incompatibility between communism and nationalism. This is contrary to the popular perception that communism does not acknowledge ethnicity because such an acknowledgement would weaken class solidarity. Lenin also consistently spoke out against antisemitism. The Soviet Union, shortly after its creation, enacted laws that made racism – including antisemitism – illegal. Moreover, the Bolsheviks set aside land in the Ukraine and Crimea for Jews who wished to return to farming, and by 1934 there were 83 Jewish collective farms in Crimea alone.[22] In 1923 the American anarchist and ardent Bolshevik sympathiser, Emma Goldman, wrote of her disappointment when she visited Russia, her sole consolation being that no pogroms had taken place under the Bolsheviks.[23]

The Provisional Government of 1917 that replaced the Duma and rule by the Romanov dynasty in Russia abolished the legal disabilities previously imposed on ethnic and religious communities, including Jews. For the first time in Russia and its empire, Jews enjoyed the same legal and political rights as other citizens. The legal restrictions on ethnic and religious communities were abolished on Wednesday, 4 April 1917, just two days before the first day of Passover, the holiday that Jews celebrate to commemorate their liberation from slavery in ancient Egypt.[24] Understandably, the abolition of these restrictions, together with the biblical symbolism of Passover, fostered the belief among Jews that antisemitism and communism were incompatible. This idea attracted many Jews – not only in Russia but around the world – to the communist cause, as did the Party's decision in 1918, to establish a Jewish or Hebrew section, known as the *Yevsektsiya* which encouraged Jews to spread the communist revolution to the Jewish masses.[25] The fact that Semyon Dimanstein, the first head of the *Yevsektsiya,* was an ordained rabbi who had studied at a yeshiva, further enhanced communism's reputation of being friendly toward the Jews. Similarly, Lenin, in his short-lived coalition with the Socialist Revolutionary Party, appointed an orthodox Jew, Isaac Steinberg, as People's Commissar of Justice. This appointment seemed to be another confirmation that the communists were not opposed to the Jews, although it was said that Lenin would lose patience with Steinberg when the Commissar refused to work on the Sabbath.[26] Jews were also drawn to communism because the forces opposed to the Bolsheviks were generally violently antisemitic and were the instigators of numerous sadistic and brutal pogroms where much Jewish blood was spilt.[27] During the Russian Civil War (1919–22) tens of thousands of Jews were murdered by anti-communist Ukrainians, and the Tsarist generals who led the White army, which was opposed to the Bolshevik or Red army, made no secret that if they won, both Bolsheviks and Jews would be exterminated.²⁸ Pogroms were perpetrated by the Bolsheviks, but the scale of these attacks was much less severe than the scale and savagery of the massacres perpetrated by their opponents.²⁹ The British academic Brendan McGeever notes that while antisemitism traversed the political divide, the Soviet leadership took active measures to prevent pogroms. For example, the Moscow Soviet organised lectures and meetings in factories on antisemitism, while in the former Pale of Settlement, local soviets were instrumental in preventing the outbreak of violence against Jews. McGeever notes that by mid-1917, the soviets had become the main focus of political opposition to antisemitism in Russia.³⁰ Indeed, with the establishment of the USSR in 1922, the new state became the only country in the world in which expressions of anti-Jewish sentiment were punished.

Before the Civil War, the Tsar's relentless antisemitism had produced many pogroms that ended the lives of countless Jews – understandably, the occurrence of such violence drew many Jews to the Bolshevik cause. The Tsar's antisemitism is illustrated in a conversation between the founder of modern Zionism, Theodor Herzl, and the Russian Finance Minister, Sergei Witte, when the two met in Saint Petersburg in 1903. Witte, who had the reputation of being more liberal than any of the Tsar's other ministers, pointed out to Herzl that while there were only seven million Jews in Russia's population of 136 million, 50 per cent of the membership of the revolutionary parties was Jewish. Herzl then asked him whose fault this was. Witte replied: 'I think it is the fault of our government. The Jews are too oppressed.'[31] Similar views were expressed by Lenin who is reported as saying that 'no nationality in Russia is as oppressed and persecuted as the Jews.'[32]

Outside Russia the Communist Party was far more accepting of religious and ethnic diversity than the traditional national parties. In Australia the CPA welcomed new immigrants by creating specific ethnic groups or branches catering for Greeks, Italians, Chinese and Jews. The other political parties, especially the ALP, the Nationalist Party of Australia and the Country Party made few overtures to attract support among non-English-speaking new arrivals.[33]

The Jewish section or faction of the CPA pandered to Jewish supporters, who, like my uncle (Yaakov Leib Mendelson) were cocooned in a totally protective society where they communicated with each other in Yiddish and where their interest was maintained through a wide array of Jewish political and cultural activities. This welcoming and comfortable environment, which did not discriminate against them and provided for all their social and political needs, made it difficult for disenchanted Jewish members to abandon the Party, which suggests that while many Jewish Party members had abandoned their religious affiliation they were not prepared to forsake their cultural heritage. It was probably for this reason that Jewish Party members stayed with communism after the 1939 Molotov–Ribbentrop Pact when Moscow formed an unprincipled alliance with the murderous antisemitic Nazis. Even after the details of Stalin's antisemitic purges emerged, many Jewish CPA members would not believe the evidence and continued to faithfully accept the story line emanating from Moscow.

On hearing of developments in post-revolutionary Russia, particularly what appeared to be its enlightened approach to minorities such as the Jews, some Jews who had left Tsarist Russia for a better life in North America and Australia decided to return to the country of their birth.[34] This group, which had concluded that the Bolsheviks represented a 'new hope' for Jews, included one member of the Komesaroff family, Clara Berchansky, who had settled in Canada in 1927, but returned to the Soviet Union in 1936 where she remained until 1962 when her mother's intensive lobbying resulted in her being allowed to re-emigrate.[35] Clara's residence in the Soviet Union during much of the Stalinist period helped maintain contacts with family who had not emigrated during the first two decades of the twentieth century after which an 'iron curtain' encompassed the country and communication with foreigners became difficult.

Until 1922, when Stalin assumed control of the Soviet Union and began to oppress its Jewish citizens and close down their cultural organisations, communist policy toward the Jews had been determined by Lenin, who took a definitive stand against antisemitism and seemed devoid of any personal racial prejudice. In 1922, the Comintern proclaimed that 'the international proletariat does not harbour any racial prejudice'.[36] During his life Lenin never indulged in anti-Jewish remarks, either in private or in public, nor did he exploit deep-rooted Russian antisemitism to advance his revolutionary cause. He repeatedly praised the role of the Jews in the revolutionary movement and was one of the most adamant and consistent in the Party in his denunciation of pogroms and antisemitism more generally.[37] He was also more inclined to support some degree of ethnic autonomy for Russia's Jewish citizens than any of his successors, especially Stalin. Lenin's policy with regard to Jewish affairs can be contrasted with that of Marx, whom Lenin believed was anti-Jewish. Despite being Jewish by birth, Marx used popular stereotypes of Jews to advance his arguments and was not beyond using the racial origins of his opponents to criticise and ridicule them. He also believed that Jews must renounce their religion as a condition of political emancipation.[38]

This positive view of Lenin does not justify his lust for power nor does it absolve him of his ruthless persecution of his own people, including Jews, if they were seen to obstruct his pursuit of a communist Russia.

In most of the world the Soviets were seen as being at the forefront of the defeat of German fascism, a perception that was reinforced by images of the Red Army occupying Berlin in May 1945 – two months ahead of their American and European allies. Furthermore, before 1939, when Stalin and Hitler had signed their non-aggression pact, communists in many countries had been at the forefront of confronting the fascist threat. In Britain, this was clearly demonstrated with their leadership, in October 1936, of the *Battle of Cable Street* where the communists organised community resistance to a proposed march through the Jewish areas of East London by Oswald Mosley's British Union of Fascists (known as the Black Shirts). The official leadership of the local Jewish community, the Board of Deputies of British Jews, denounced the march as antisemitic and urged all Jews to remain indoors and not be provoked by the Black Shirts.[39] Warnings were also issued from synagogue pulpits, and posters in similar terms were plastered on walls adjoining the proposed march.[40]

Many of the district's Jews felt abandoned by what they perceived as the passivity and weakness of their community's leadership, so they were readily co-opted by the communists to join a multi-racial group of anti-fascists who confronted and thoroughly routed Mosley and his thugs. Subsequently, at the next local and national elections, many of the communists – a number of whom were Jewish – who had organised the resistance to the Black Shirts, campaigned under the communist banner for parliamentary and council positions and were elected comfortably. This support for the communist cause suggests that it had little to do with Marxism and was more a consequence of the fact that the communists were seen to be the only effective resistance to fascism.[41]

In Australia, until well into the 1950s, the local Communist Party followed Lenin's policy by consistently opposing antisemitism because they believed that it distracted the attention of workers from the evils of capitalism and thereby weakened the labour movement.[42] In a 1944 file note, one of ASIO's forerunners, the Commonwealth Investigation Service (CIS), took a less sophisticated and more pragmatic view when it attributed Jewish support for communist causes to 'the belief that Russia would assist the Jewish race as a whole in obtaining cancellation of the ... British White Paper ... which provided for a complete cessation of [Jewish] immigration into Palestine ...'[43]

Most, if not all, of the CPA's Jewish adherents were passionate supporters of Israel, and Moscow's rapid recognition of the Jewish state after its founding in May 1948 would have reinforced their belief that the Soviet Union was a committed friend of the Jews.[44] The Soviet Union was the third nation to recognise Israel – the United States and Guatemala had recognised Israel three days earlier, but this was *de facto* recognition, whereas the Soviet Union was the first country to grant *de jure* recognition.[45] In addition to providing diplomatic support, Moscow instructed its communist satellite, Czechoslovakia, to supply military equipment to the Jewish Agency; this was crucial to Israel's success in the 1948 Arab-Israeli War. The Soviet Union's diplomatic and military support for the State of Israel (which was in marked contrast with the regime's negative attitude to Zionism) was driven by Stalin's belief that the new country's leaders, many of whom were born in Russia and Eastern Europe, were socialists and that they would align Israel with the communist camp. With Israel as a political ally, Stalin expected to gain a diplomatic foothold in the Middle East and so hasten the decline of British dominance in this oil-rich region.[46]

Some Jewish supporters of communism were attracted by the Party's economic philosophies, but I believe that this was much less of an attraction than the Party's apparent support for Israel and opposition to all forms of racism, especially antisemitism. This is not to suggest that the Party's Jewish adherents were not supporters of communism's claim to seek a more equitable society, but I would argue this issue was very much secondary to the Party's perceived opposition to antisemitism. Support for the Party's economic policies was seen by many of its Jewish members as an incidental cost to be borne because of the Party's support for racial equality. Certainly I am of the firm view that, among its Jewish members, support for the Party's policy of abolition of private property was negligible. This is especially the case with the members of my family who were members of the CPA or were active participants in front organisations. For the most part they were relatively prosperous small-business people who were extremely philanthropic, but who resigned from the Party and various front organisations when it became obvious that the communists were not serious in their support for a Jewish homeland or in their opposition to antisemitism.

Many Jews believed that the Soviet Union was a utopia

that had emancipated its Jewish citizens – what Philip Mendes describes as 'the powerful belief that the Soviet Union was good for the Jews' – so it is understandable that the newly-formed JCCFA welcomed support from the CPA and its members.[47] However, aside from Judah Waten, who had been expelled from the CPA and was the Council's first paid organiser, its foundation Executive Committee did not include any communists.[48] Waten had been expelled in 1942 for advocating a government of national unity to defeat fascism, but rejoined in 1956: a time when many were leaving the CPA in protest over the Soviet invasion of Hungary. Despite his expulsion, for most of his life Waten was a staunch Marxist who blindly supported Stalin's policies, even when evidence of the dictator's crimes was obvious. In 1960, when Soviet excesses had become known outside Russia, particularly toward its Jewish citizens, Waten claimed that 'the revolution of 1917 had liberated Jews from Czarist bondage' and Soviet antisemitism 'was a lie invented by the Anglo-American propaganda machine who were the real organisers of Anti-semitism'.[49]

The Australian government's reaction to an article in the 28 January 1949 issue of the *Jewish Herald* shows how Waten's involvement with the Council actually harmed the cause of combating antisemitism. The article referred to an advertisement in the secular press that threatened to publish the names of Jewish property holders so that they would be harassed by antisemites. The article came to the attention of the head of the CIS in Canberra, who instructed his Melbourne office to seek more information on the threat. When agents in Melbourne identified Waten as the author of the *Jewish Herald* article they responded to Canberra's request with the comment 'that it would not appear politic to approach him'.[50]

While the JCCFA was criticised by some conservative Anglo-Jews who disapproved of its high and proactive public profile, the Council was remarkably successful, because it was able to unify a Jewish community that was concerned by the antisemitic policies of right-wing regimes. The fact that the JCCFA was able to reach out for support from sympathisers beyond its own religious compatriots added to its influence, and within two years of its creation the Council had been appointed to manage the public relations activities of Victoria's peak Jewish organisation – the Jewish Advisory Board.[51]

The Council's fortunes began to change in 1949 with the onset of the Cold War and with increased awareness of state-sponsored antisemitism so that Jewish communities behind the Iron Curtain did not feel secure. The Soviets had also begun to modify their perceived strong pro-Jewish and pro-Israel policies.[52] At the same time, Australian politicians began to draw attention to the number of CPA members who had influence on the Council, which, they concluded, showed that the JCCFA was most likely a communist front organisation. This view is supported by ASIO's files for the early 1950s, which show that some of the Council's staff and supporters were resigning because they were also concerned over a growing communist influence. Its agents within the Council reported to ASIO that Hyam Wittner and his wife (Dora) ceased their donations after several years because of infiltration of the Council by communists.[53]

In his 1968 sociological study of the Melbourne Jewish community, Peter Medding argues that, while the Council was composed of a large cross-section of the community and it remained united in its fight against antisemitism and support for the creation of a Jewish state, it had, nonetheless, been infiltrated by a number of avowed communists and fellow travellers. These people had achieved key positions within the organisation, so they were able to influence its policies in accordance with their political views.[54]

The Jewish community's opposition to the Commonwealth government's 1950 plan to resettle non-Jewish displaced Germans in Australia further damaged the Council's reputation and contributed to its demise. Fearing that many of the proposed settlers would be neo-fascist antisemites who had actively served the Third Reich, the community lobbied the newly elected Menzies Liberal government to abandon this resettlement policy. However, German migration was not an issue for most Australians and this was confirmed by ASIO, who advised the government that only two groups were opposed to the resettlement proposal: Jewish organisations, which were incensed by Germany's conduct in the Holocaust, and the CPA, which viewed the proposed new arrivals as strongly anti-communist.[55] ASIO raised no objections to these people applying for citizenship and praised them for their anti-communism, while ignoring the war criminals among them who had left a murderous trail when they migrated from Europe.[56] Despite its seeming inability to differentiate between genuine refugees and war criminals, ASIO had correctly assessed the mood of the wider Australian community, where 65 per cent of those polled were in favour of German migration, a higher proportion than those who supported other non-English-speaking migrants.[57]

Armed with ASIO's assessment Harold Holt, the Minister for Immigration, responded to the Jewish community's pressure by threatening to prevent the transfer of any funds to Israel and to freeze the bank accounts of local Zionist organisations.[58] Holt's threat was enough to stop wider community protests, but the JCCFA persisted, which led to it being seen as a communal embarrassment and claims that its opposition was politically motivated and designed to help the communists. Indeed, a major criticism levelled against the Council was that it was more concerned with defending communism than it was in promoting the interests of Melbourne's Jewish community.[59] In 1993, a quarter of a century after it had ceased to operate, one of JCCFA's communist founders, Lou Jedwab, had come to the conclusion that one reason for the Council's demise was that it continued to defend 'the USSR when it was no longer defendable'.[60] Another of the Council's founders, Norman Rothfield, reminisced that he had 'mistakenly temporised over condemnation of antisemitism in communist countries'.⁶¹

Because the JCCFA had close affiliations with left-leaning (including communist) groups and individuals, the charge of being a front organisation was particularly damaging and was the basis for ASIO initiating surveillance of the Council and its leaders.⁶² Ultimately, the belief that the Council had become a front for the CPA resulted in it being expelled from the Victorian Jewish Board of Deputies (VJBD) and proscribed by the Victorian branch of the ALP in 1952.⁶³

For a time after the expulsion of the JCCFA from the VJBD, when dealing with government departments or ministers, communal organisations such as the Executive Council of Australian Jewry (ECAJ) would emphasise that the JCCFA represented 'a very small minority group of people' and that many of the leadership were members of the CPA.⁶⁴ As a consequence of Cold War hysteria, such communal sensitivity to communism extended beyond the ECAJ and even included Melbourne's prestigious Mount Scopus College, Australia's first Jewish day school, whose policy was not to hire teaching staff, even Jewish teachers, who were or had been members of the CPA. This prohibition applied irrespective of the teacher's qualifications or experience, but did not apply to donors or the board of governors, some of whom were extremely generous benefactors to the College, but were well known to ASIO.

The extreme left-wing organisation Gezerd was another Australian group which, like the JCCFA had been modelled on a Soviet organisation of the same name. Gezerd, an acronym for the Yiddish translation of 'Society for the Settlement of Jewish Toilers on the Land in the USSR', was established in Moscow in 1925 with the aim of promoting the settlement of Jews in Birobidzhan, a desolate area in the far eastern part of the Soviet Union, near the border with China. The intention was that Jews in Birobidzhan would have their own administrative, educational and judicial institutions and that these institutions would function in their own language – Yiddish.[65] No Jews had ever lived in the area; however, as Richard Overy reports in his book *Russia's War*, Soviet propaganda made great play with the idea that in Birobidzhan the regime was protecting the culture and identity of the Jewish people.[66]

The renowned authority on Jewish history and on the history of socialism and Marxism, Chimen Abramsky, points out that, despite the Soviet propaganda, the Birobidzhan project was not a Jewish initiative. Instead, it originated from the People's Commissariat of Agriculture, and was strongly supported by the Commissariat of Defence and the Agricultural Academy, institutions that were motivated more by national security issues than by any compassion for the country's Jewish population. Many prominent Soviet Jews, including the leadership of Gezerd, strongly opposed the scheme on the grounds that the Birobidzhan climate was harsh and the soil was unsuitable for cultivation. Instead, they proposed creating a Jewish republic in Crimea.[67]

Though it ultimately failed in its goal of creating a Jewish homeland in Russia, the Birobidzhan project was important for Soviet propaganda purposes and the Soviets used its existence as an argument against Zionism, an ideology that rivalled Marxism among gullible left-wing Jews.[68] On the other hand, many Zionists, including members of the Komesaroff clan in Australia, saw Birobidzhan as a contingency plan, should their efforts at creating a Jewish state in the Holy Land fail.

The first Australian branch of Gezerd was established in Melbourne in May 1930 by a group of Eastern European Jews which included my uncle, Yaakov Leib Mendelson, and his non-communist cousin Peter Komesaroff. Many of the founders, including my uncle, had been members of the Jewish Socialist Group and the Kadimah Yiddish Culture Group, organisations that catered to secular, though Zionistic, Jews from eastern Europe, who at the time were reshaping Jewish communities around Australia. Described by Malcolm J. Turnbull as 'a fearlessly Stalinist "satellite" group', most of Gezerd's members in Melbourne were also members of Kadimah, but wanted to create a less diverse, more Soviet-oriented organisation free of influence from their political opponents – the secular and staunchly anti-communist workers party, the Bund.[69, 70] In breaking with Kadimah the Australian arm of Gezerd wanted to 'spread proletarian culture among the Jews of Melbourne; to assist in the reconstruction of Jewish life in the USSR; and to work with fraternal organisations in the defence of the USSR.' From a local perspective Gezerd claimed to stand 'for a solution to Jewish problems, which are national in form and socialist in content.'[71] Though it was an organisation of Jews, Gezerd was vehemently opposed to Jewish religious practice and was often critical of their observant religious cohorts, describing them as 'reactionary' and 'chauvinistic' people who fabricated lies about the life and achievements of Jews in the Soviet Union.

Gezerd was never popular with the conservative Anglo segment of Australia's Jewish community, who described it as a 'Jewish secret society', whose members were 'lacking in restraint and discretion' and were an 'undesirable foreign element.'[72] In April 1933, Gezerd's Victorian Branch convened a public meeting to register their concern with the appalling plight of the Jewish citizens of Germany, and while the communal leadership endorsed the meeting's objectives, it felt the need to place advertisements in Melbourne's daily newspapers announcing that the meeting had 'not been organised by the Victorian Jewish community.'[73]

Despite its rejection by the waning Anglo-Jewish establishment, by the mid-1930s Gezerd in Melbourne boasted several hundred members, and in 1938 it opened a reading room and lending library – Culture House – at 717 Rathdowne Street, Carlton. During this period, despite its differences with the Bund, it formed a coalition with that group in the common fight against European fascism and antisemitism. This alliance broke down in 1939 with the Molotov-Ribbentrop Pact, when the Nazis and Soviets signed a non-aggression pact, and after this Gezerd's membership declined rapidly until its demise in 1944.[74]

Gezerd's political sympathies were very much in evidence in 1934 when Egon Kisch, a Czechoslovakia-born Jewish member of the Comintern, visited Australia to attend an anti-fascist conference. Canberra's refusal to allow Kisch to enter Australia resulted in protests organised by the CPA and these protests included representatives of Gezerd. These demonstrations usually concluded with the singing of the *Internationale*, a socialist movement hymn, which was also the national anthem of the Soviet Union.[75] Kisch was finally permitted to enter Australia, and Gezerd hosted him at a meeting in Sydney, where its leaders berated the local press for promulgating anti-Jewish tales of life in the Soviet Union, which they claimed were the work of Stalin's arch enemy, the Jewish-born Leon Trotsky.[76] Another example of Jewish communists demonstrating that their Party affiliation was far more important than their identity as Jews.

Because Gezerd was a strong supporter of the Soviet Union, its members were under regular surveillance by the IB, which opened a file on the organisation in January 1931, just months after the group was formed.[77] Initially the local security authorities were uncertain of how to treat Gezerd, which seemed to have no fixed rules or regulations governing membership, but they regarded it as 'an interesting addition to the propaganda units established by the communist movement'. After extensive correspondence with their MI5 colleagues in London, the people at the IB concluded that, apart from the pro-communist inclinations of its leadership, 'there does not appear any reason to consider this organisation to be of security interest'. Despite concluding that Gezerd was not a security threat, IB continued to monitor the organisation and record its activities on an ever-expanding file.

While Gezerd was not seen as a risk to security, the group did incur the wrath of Commonwealth authorities because it failed to obtain approval from the Department of External Affairs for its publication, *New World*. Federal regulations of the time required publishers of newspapers and journals that included large tracts of foreign language material to obtain prior approval from Canberra. Much of *New World* was printed in Yiddish, and despite several reminders, Gezerd's leadership never sought approval for their publication.

Most of *New World*'s Yiddish copy was reprinted from overseas publications. One of the frequent foreign contributors went by the name Shlomo Yitzchaki, and the security authorities assumed he was an American-based rabbi. As would be recognised by observant Jews, Rabbi Shlomo Yitzchaki was the name of a prominent medieval Jewish scholar known today by the acronym *Rashi,* and in this case the name was probably a pen-name for an author who wanted to remain anonymous. This possibility did not seem to occur to the IB's agents.

The last entry on Gezerd's file is dated September 1944, by which time the group was in terminal decline.

ASIO and its predecessors also maintained files on other Jewish organisations, including the Bund, Kadimah, *Youth Aliyah*, the Jewish Welfare and Relief Society as well as Jewish youth groups.[78] The Kadimah organisation attracted ASIO's interest because many of its members were communists and it permitted its hall in Carlton to be used for CPA functions. These other organisations are not discussed here because only a few of their records have been released by ASIO and none seem to refer to any of the 44 members of the Komesaroff family covered by this study.[79]

4

The Seven Files on Komesaroff Family Members

As Australia's counter-intelligence services evolved and earlier agencies were replaced by newer ones, files were culled and documents regarded as no longer relevant were destroyed. For example, when ASIO relocated its head office from Sydney to Melbourne in 1950, there was an extensive rationalisation of records, and files dating back to the early 1920s were destroyed. I am of the firm view that such destruction was not a deliberate policy for disposing of 'incriminating evidence', but was, rather, a practical policy for minimising the cost of file relocation and storage. Also, as people died, their files were destroyed; files that were not destroyed were later transferred to succeeding agencies, and it is through this process that ASIO holds some documents that predate its creation. Apart from culling obsolete records, it would appear that on its creation ASIO did not inherit all the files from its predecessor organisations, as some of them were 'lost' or 'misplaced'.[1] The first Hope Royal Commission describes the time when ASIO took over from the Commonwealth

Investigation Service (CIS) as 'a bitter period'. CIS people regarded the contacts they developed as 'personal assets', whose details they assumed they could take with them, along with their own 'personal files', on leaving the organisation. The Commission's report mentions that at least one CIS investigator retained his 'personal files' and did not transfer them to ASIO.[2] The hostility between the CIS and ASIO continued into the 1960s when the former body was absorbed into the Commonwealth Police. The antagonism between the CIS and ASIO may explain why the dossiers relating to members of the Komesaroff clan appear to be incomplete.

In his official history of ASIO, John Blaxland reports that the organisation's records management had serious deficiencies, lacking adequate systems for storage and retrieval and for controlling access to information. 'File documents often lacked details including numbers, descriptions, dates and signatures. Such oversights made control and audit of records all the more difficult.'[3] The premature and unauthorised shredding of nineteen files relating to Gerontiy Pavlovich Lazovik, the Soviet Committee for State Security (KGB) resident (1974 to 1977) and First Secretary at the Soviet Embassy in Canberra, is a perfect example of the consequences of ASIO's dysfunctional filing system. In 1980, ASIO received information that Lazovik had been awarded a medal for an intelligence recruitment while he was stationed in Australia. Hoping to identify the Australian traitor, ASIO called up their files on Lazovik but were horrified to learn that the documents had been destroyed.

In my examination of well over 200 files that ASIO has released, I have found that the files share two common characteristics. Firstly, most files were opened in response to a perceived specific threat, but when the threat was found to be no longer credible, the file was not closed and information continued to be collected, creating an ever-expanding file. Such information collection has made many files voluminous, although they seem to contain little information of national security value.

The second characteristic of ASIO's files that I noted was that they expanded beyond the scope of their initial target. An example of this is a file on Zionist youth organisations that was created as a result of an intercepted letter from a communist, Frances Bernie, to the Secretary of the Cambridge University Labour Federation. In the letter Bernie claimed that the communist youth group, the Eureka Youth League, had established a branch known as Shomrim Zionist Youth. Bernie, who had been raised a Catholic, did not understand that communists only represented a small proportion of the Shomrim Zionist movement, but, based on her intercepted letter, ASIO opened a file on the Shomrim and this file ultimately became a large repository for information on all of Australia's Zionist youth groups.[4]

ASIO's dysfunctional filing system came as a surprise, because when the organisation was formed in 1949, it was modeled on MI5, Britain's domestic counter-intelligence and security agency, and several British agents were sent to Australia to assist their Commonwealth colleagues. The new organisation's record-keeping arrangements were copied directly from MI5's central file registry, and adapted where necessary for local conditions.[5]

In Australia access to archival records is governed by the *Archives Act* 1983. Under the Act, Commonwealth government records are released for access by the public when they reach what is known as the 'open-access period'. Depending on when the document was generated the open-access period ranges from 20 to 30 years after it was created. Through the National Archives of Australia (NAA) I requested files from ASIO of all the 44 first- and second-generation Komesaroff family members in Australia. ASIO was able to confirm that they had files on only seven members of my family, and at my request, these seven dossiers were transferred to the NAA.

The transfer process precludes blanket applications for families or other groups and requires a separate request for each individual or organisation. There were only three instances when I was surprised that ASIO's archivists were not able to locate all the files I sought. The first of these involved Cecilia Nathan (née Komisaruk), who came to Australia in 1912 to marry David Zmood. Cecilia was known to be very active in left-wing politics and during the Great War she is alleged to have encouraged her husband (David Zmood) to flee to America to avoid conscription.[6] A number of family members have claimed she was an ardent member of the CPA, so I had expected to find a file labelled with her name. However, in 1928 Cecilia's marriage ended in a bitter divorce and she changed her name several times subsequently, which may have made it difficult to locate a file in 2017. It is also possible that the Commonwealth Investigation Branch (CIB), another forerunner of ASIO, had a file on Cecilia and when the CIB's functions were absorbed by ASIO the document was destroyed because it was regarded as no longer relevant.

I had also expected a file on Cecilia's daughter (Tybel, who lived with her mother), but none was located. Several people who knew her told me that Tybel had been a member of the CPA. Unless ASIO staff have conspired to prevent my access to the file, which I do not believe, it is more than likely the file was either misplaced or destroyed when Tybel died in 1973. People familiar with ASIO's records management give credence to the possibility of misplaced or destroyed files and describe a system with 'serious deficiencies, lacking an adequate system for storage and retrieval …'[7]

I was also disappointed that I could not locate a file relating to myself. In my youth I had been active in student politics, including opposition to conscription and the Vietnam War, and for a period in the 1980s my work required me to travel regularly to the Soviet Union. Also, at different periods in the 1990s, my employment necessitated that I live in communist China and post-communist Russia. It is possible that my opposition to the Vietnam War was less relevant and noteworthy than I had believed, and as for my trips to the Soviet Union, this information could remain embargoed by the NAA's 30-year open-access period.[8] It is also possible that my unfulfilled expectations reflect my paranoia.

While there is no personal file on me, I do feature in a file that records ASIO intercepts of telephone communications with the Soviet Embassy in Canberra.

The absence of a personal file on me reminds me of a story told by my friend, the late Stephen Murray-Smith, a former communist who resigned from the Party in 1958. In 1982 Stephen applied to the newly elected Cain Labor government in Victoria for a copy of his Special Branch file.[9] Race Mathews, a close friend of Stephen's and the Minister for Police and Emergency Services, reported that the State's Special Branch had claimed not to have a file on the former CPA member. Stephen's response was to ask Mathews not to tell anyone there was no file, as in the circles in which he moved, not to have a file would send a message that could cause him long-term problems. Around the same time, Stephen's friend, the social commentator and another former communist, Phillip Adams, had requested his ASIO file. When told 'you don't have a file', Phillip began to question the organisation's competence.[10]

The seven personal dossiers and the other 60 or so files relating to the Melbourne Jewish community and its association with the local CPA branch that I examined were devoid of gratuitous racist comments that others, who have researched the same historical period, have reported. I never encountered the crude antisemitic rants that Mark Aarons found littered throughout his family's files.[11] Aarons is not alone in suggesting that ASIO has an antisemitic streak; in his unofficial history of ASIO, Frank Cain claims that in the 1950s, 'ASIO was markedly antisemitic partly reflecting the British campaign against Jewish terrorist fighters in Palestine.'[12] None of the files I examined showed evidence of such discrimination.

The subjects of the seven ASIO files on the Komesaroff family are three first-generation migrants and four of the second generation who were born in Australia. The political beliefs of the seven ranged across the left wing of the political spectrum, from social democrat to one, but possibly two, card-carrying members of the CPA. For the most part, the seven were proud Zionists and avid opponents of antisemitism. Their religious observance spanned the range from non-observant through Liberal or Reform Judaism to traditional or orthodox Jews who maintained kosher homes and attended synagogue regularly. None of the seven held derogatory or self-hating views of Jewish people, nor were any of them apostates who had renounced Judaism. They all married Jewish partners, and with the exception of one who was cremated without any ceremony, they were all buried with acknowledgement and in accordance with their Judaism.[13]

Like their other first- and second-generation family cohorts, the seven were well integrated into Australian society, being members of non-Jewish community organisations as well as Jewish groups. While the three first-generation members of the group spoke Yiddish, they did not speak it regularly, preferring to communicate in English which they spoke fluently. The four second-generation members of the group did not speak Yiddish, but probably had some understanding of the language.

None of the seven was radical either by temperament or by conviction, and although they worked for social and political change, none of their actions could be considered radical or revolutionary. Generally they were middle-class owners of small businesses who had no affiliation with organisations such as trade unions. Five of the seven had tertiary qualifications, four in science and one in the humanities.

The educational qualifications remind me of a conclusion drawn by a Canadian Royal Commission which, in 1946, examined fourteen Canadian citizens who had betrayed their country to the Soviet Union. The Commission's analysis showed that most of the fourteen, including highly regarded scientists, were of unusually high educational standard.[14] The ASIO files on my seven relatives make it abundantly clear that they were not remotely involved in any treachery or threat to Australia; nonetheless, their preference for science and their high educational attainment are worth noting.

None of the seven is alive today, so I have not been able to discuss their records with them, though in each case I provided copies of the documents to surviving close family members, usually their children or grandchildren. In almost every case, the family member was surprised to learn of the existence of the file, but they were not necessarily shocked by the contents, though they expressed surprise that a government could spend taxpayer's money on such mundane data collection that did not seem to have any relevance to national security. In his official history of ASIO, David Horner echoes this view when he writes that it is now clear that ASIO's wide-ranging surveillance 'and the gathering of information into voluminous files, was a massive waste of time and resources.'[15]

All the files relating to members of the Komesaroff family are relatively slim, with none exceeding 124 pages – embarrassingly small when compared with the 88 volumes totalling 14,000 pages that ASIO compiled on the CPA's national secretary, Laurie Aarons. Also, with a mere seven files, the Komesaroff family pale into insignificance alongside the four generations of the Aarons dynasty that dominated the CPA and on whom, over five decades, ASIO created more than 209 files containing in excess of 32,000 pages.[16]

Details of the seven Komesaroff personal files are summarised in Table 2, which reports the size of each file, the number of redacted pages and the number of pages that were totally withheld. In Tessa Silberberg's file, as an example, the NAA reported that, for the open-access period, her file contained seven folios, of which three were released without any censorship while four included some form of redaction. For the open-access period, all seven files generated a total of 190 folios, none of which was totally exempt, although 54 contained portions that were blacked out.

Table 2: Details of the seven Komesaroff family members' ASIO files released by the NAA.

Name	Totally Exempt	Open With Exemption	Open and Transferred to NAA	Total Number of Folios in the Open-access Period
Yaakov Leib Mendelson	0	3	8	11
Myer Nathan	0	3	7	10
Peter Komesaroff	0	6	1	7
Louis Komesaroff	0	20	104	124
Max Komesaroff	0	14	13	27
Tessa Silberberg	0	4	3	7
Morris Komesaroff	0	4	0	4
Total	0	54	136	190

5
Yaakov Leib Mendelson[1]

My uncle, Yaakov Leib Mendelson, who was born in Grafskoy in 1888 and came to Australia in 1914, was an early, although not a founding member of the CPA.[2] The Party was formed in 1920 and he joined in 1929, before the rise of Hitler and at a time of global economic uncertainty. From the time of his arrival in Australia, Yaakov Leib operated as a small shopkeeper, mainly in Ballarat, but in 1928 he was declared a bankrupt and moved from Ballarat to Melbourne. At this time, probably because of the stigma of the bankruptcy, he changed his name, from Komesarook to Mendelson. He selected this name because his father's name had been Mendel and he was the son of Mendel, hence Mendelson.

Mendelson, like Komesarook, was obviously a foreign name in Australia and I have often wondered why, when Yaakov Leib changed his name, he chose to adopt another foreign name rather than adopting an Anglo-sounding surname.

He was not the first son of a Mendel to change his name to Mendelson. In the late eighteenth century the German Jewish philosopher Moses Mendelssohn (1729–86) adopted the surname Mendelssohn because he felt that his obviously Jewish name, Moses Mendel Dessau, would limit his opportunities in later life.[3] He was an active member of the Jewish community at a time when there was almost complete cultural separation between Jews and Germans. Nonetheless, Mendelssohn campaigned for emancipation and civil rights for his co-religionists, aiming to take them out of their ghetto lifestyle into secular society. He instructed Jews to form bonds with the gentile governments of the various German states. He also sought to improve relationships between Jews and Christians, arguing for tolerance and humanity.[4] These views readily accorded with those of the son of Mendel in this book, my uncle Yaakov Leib Mendelson.

Despite his prodigious intellect, Mendelssohn the philosopher did not have any formal education, apart from his Jewish studies. His first language was Yiddish and he taught himself German, Latin, Greek, French and English, as well as mathematics, logic and philosophy. All this was achieved through reading every book he could find.[5] Similarly, more than 100 years later in Australia, Yaakov Leib Mendelson, whose first language was also Yiddish, taught himself English by avidly reading local newspapers. His fierce intellect was further developed through his intensive reading of books on topics ranging from Jewish humour to political philosophy which he accumulated in his vast library.

Yaakov Leib Mendelson was an avowed atheist who rarely attended synagogue, whereas Moses Mendelson maintained strict observance of Jewish law throughout his life and never deviated from it. Despite this difference, it is quite likely that when Yaakov Leib Komesarook wanted to change his name, his choice of Mendelson was influenced by the actions of the German philosopher, who, as a central figure in the Jewish Enlightenment, campaigned for civil rights for Jews – actions that Yaakov Leib Komesarook would certainly have strongly admired and endorsed.

So committed was Yaakov Leib to the communist cause that he commissioned a terrazzo tile floor featuring a hammer and sickle for the side porch of his Melbourne home. His wife, Bessie, embarrassed by her husband's politics, tried to conceal the symbol with a strategically placed doormat, but she was not successful, as the feature was too large.[6]

The 1929 date for Yaakov Leib's joining of the CPA is consistent with reports cited by David Rechter which said that around this time Yaakov Leib was an active participant in left-wing organisations, including the Jewish Socialist Group and Gezerd.[7] Later he was prominent in the leadership of the Jewish fraction of the CPA, as well as being active in the International Association of Friends of the Soviet Union and the Australia-Soviet Friendship League.[8] Further confirmation that Yaakov Leib joined the CPA in 1929 comes from a letter he wrote in March 1946 to the *Australian Jewish News*, where he claimed to have been a member of the Party for seventeen years.[9] However, his diaries and the reminiscences of contemporaries

Fig. 6: Yaakov Leib Mendelson, circa 1920.

would suggest that Yaakov Leib had harboured strong left-leaning views from an early age. During his early years in Australia Yaakov Leib recorded his thoughts and experiences in a diary, making it clear that he was loyal to the communist cause even before 1914 when he left Grafskoy, and his later experiences only sharpened his commitment. On his return journey to Europe in 1921 to reconnect with the family, Yaakov Leib wrote that, having boarded the ship, he went down to the third-class cabins:

> ... to find my equals and here you can see the capitalist might, even without glasses ... Here I met the Russian working class, who after a long exile, in Australia or New Zealand, in the mines and sugar plantations, who didn't have any rights under the previous regime, even the right to go home, now they carry their parcels to the free Bolshevik Government.[10]

I find it hard to reconcile the writer of these words with the person who campaigned tenaciously, against very high odds, to enable his own family to come to Australia from Russia. If Yaakov Leib had truly believed the Bolsheviks offered freedom, why did he lobby the Australian government for passports for his family, as it would have been much easier for him to return to live in Russia?

Another aspect of my uncle's early years in Australia that I find surprising is that from around 1917, when he began to petition to have his family granted approval to come to Australia, until 1922, when they arrived here, he seems to have suppressed his long-held admiration for the communist cause. During this period there was a hiatus in his contributions to socialist newspapers and he did not join the Party until 1929. I have formed the view that while he was lobbying for entry permits for his family, Yaakov Leib's public statements were designed to appeal to Australian officials who, at that time, were fearful of communist influence and opposed issuing entry permits to Russian nationals.

While Yaakov Leib may have wanted to conceal his radical views so as to protect his alien status, he appears to have let his guard down in 1919, when he wrote a short piece on antisemitism for the Sydney magazine *The International Socialist*.[11] Despite this lapse, his pretence seems to have been successful, because in May 1921 the government issued entry permits for the family.[12] However, my uncle's reports to the Australian press, on meeting the family across the border from Russia, were critical of the terrible situation in the country of his birth.[13] His criticism prompted another Sydney publication, *The Communist*, to label Yaakov Leib as someone who, while in Australia 'found it to be quite easy to pass as a revolutionist of a sort', but the closer the 'shopkeeper from Ballarat' came to Russia, 'the nearer he got to Kerensky'.[14] The article then challenged 'the small shopkeeper' to inform them 'through the capitalist press exactly what changed his mind'.[15]

As a high-profile CPA member of seventeen years' standing, it is not surprising that Yaakov Leib attracted the attention of Australia's security services. However, what is surprising is that the file they kept on him is remarkably thin – a mere eleven pages – and it covers only the last few years of his life.[16] I suspect another earlier file may have been created by ASIO's predecessor, the Commonwealth Investigation Service (CIS) and for the reasons explained in chapter 3, it was not transferred to ASIO when that organisation was established.

The information contained in Yaakov Leib's file is mostly mundane – much of it extracted from electoral rolls, newspaper articles and other public documents. An index card in the file records that in 1946 my uncle was Secretary of the Jewish Branch of the CPA and that in 1944 he was a member of the Jewish Council to Combat Fascism and Anti-Semitism (JCCFA). The same card notes; '… during the war years he was active in importing Russian literature' and was president of the 'Jews [sic] Group – Russian Br. [Branch] Aust. [Australian] Red Cross.' Yaakov Leib's association with the Red Cross was hardly a secret, as it was reported in the daily newspapers when he and Bessie hosted a card party to raise funds for the Melbourne Lord Mayor's Russian Relief Fund.[17] Similarly, his importation of Russian literature, including Russian and Yiddish editions of *Einigkeit*, the Jewish anti-Fascist Committee (JAFC) newspaper, was well known through advertisements he placed in newspapers such as the Melbourne *Argus* (see Figure 5).[18]

Yaakov Leib's file records that in June 1948 he paid £10 for a subscription to *The Tribune*, the official CPA newspaper.[19] A file notation states that the information was obtained from a receipt book that the authorities had acquired in July 1949 when they raided *Marx House*, the CPA's Sydney headquarters. That a self-declared member

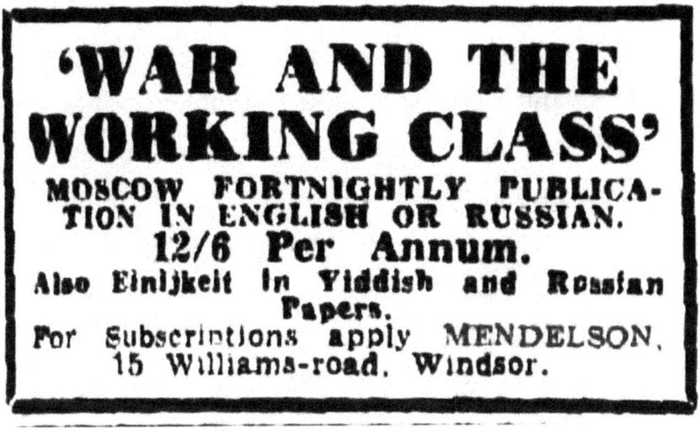

> **'WAR AND THE WORKING CLASS'**
> MOSCOW FORTNIGHTLY PUBLICATION IN ENGLISH OR RUSSIAN.
> **12/6 Per Annum.**
> Also Einljkeit in Yiddish and Russian Papers.
> For Subscriptions apply MENDELSON, 15 Williams-road, Windsor.

Fig. 5: Advertisement for Russian publications placed by Yaakov Leib Mendelson in the Melbourne *Argus*, 6 June 1945, p. 4. *Einigkeit* was a periodical published by the Soviet Jewish anti-Fascist Committee (JAFC). *War and Working Class* was another Soviet publication.

of the CPA would subscribe to *The Tribune* would hardly be a secret, but this subscription does come as a shock to me, because Yaakov Leib had broken with the Party two years earlier, in March 1946.

Yaakov Leib's file has another unexpected revelation – his membership of the radical New Zionist Organization. This organisation and their youth group, Betar, followed the teachings of Vladimir Jabotinsky, a controversial right-wing Zionist who some have labelled as a fascist. A staunch anti-communist who opposed the socialist orientation of mainstream Zionism, Jabotinsky advocated violence as a means of establishing a Jewish State that would occupy both sides of the Jordan River. Given Yaakov-Leib's strong socialist and pacifist beliefs, it is surprising that he could muster the political agility to support a movement whose philosophical leader was a right-wing anti-socialist advocate of violence. It is possible that ASIO may have confused my uncle with someone else with a similar name, but as Yaakov-Leib's subsequent resignation from the CPA illustrates, Zionism was far more important to him than communism, so it is possible that the reference could be to him.

Although Yaakov Leib's personal file is thin, the file opened by ASIO on the CPA's interests and activities in the Jewish community is far more revealing about his work and what motivated him to join the Party and other left-leaning groups.[20] The file has numerous examples of the ways in which the Party sought to infiltrate Jewish organisations by emphasising communist opposition to antisemitism and describing how Soviet troops were sacrificing themselves to destroy the antisemitic fascists. The first page of the file is a closely typed document stating the 'Tasks of Jewish communists in the struggle against Anti-semitism and for the rights of the Jewish people', which was published toward the end of World War II and was somehow intercepted by ASIO. The document is essentially a call to arms for Jewish communists to campaign within the wider Jewish community about the evils of antisemitism. The document argues that, with the War coming to an end, reactionary forces will emerge that will use the evils of antisemitism to sow discord between all elements of society, the implication of these statements being that antisemitism is a tool used by the capitalists to deflect attention from their own actions by creating disharmony within the working class.[21]

For a world that was just beginning to realise the full horrors of the Nazi Holocaust, communism, which preached freedom and equality, appealed to many Jews, especially those who, like my uncle, were more secular than religious. Except for a brief period, the communists had always challenged the Nazis and they seemed sincere in their condemnation of race hatred, so it is understandable why many Jews, my uncle included, were attracted to communism, which seemed to respect Jews and our culture, and it is for this reason that the Investigation Branch (IB) description of Yaakov Leib, in 1943, as 'extremely active in any matters concerning Soviet Russia to which country he has a deep and abiding attachment' rings true.

The ASIO file on the CPA's activities in the Jewish community makes it abundantly clear that Yaakov Leib had 'a dominant personality' and was an indefatigable worker supporting the communist cause and opposing antisemitism. He is also referred to as being influential in the Victorian Branch of the CPA.[22] Yaakov Leib was co-chairman of the Russian Aid and Comforts Committee, which raised money for the Jewish community of Kuybyshev (now known as Samara), Russia's sixth-largest city. With fewer than 10,000 Jews, Kuybyshev had a relatively small Jewish population, but its attraction for Australia's Jewish comrades was that during World War II it was the headquarters of the Soviet JAFC.

Selling subscriptions to newspapers and periodicals

such as *Moscow News*, *Pravda*, *Izvestia* and *Patriotic War* helped raise funds for the Kuybyshev project, but also drew the attention of Australia's counter-intelligence service. When briefed on this fundraising in March 1943, the Minister for Immigration, Arthur Calwell, recommended that the IB take action to monitor the donated money, because he believed that, rather than going to Russia, the money would most likely be diverted to communist propaganda in Australia.[23]

Unaware of government concerns that the proceeds of his sales of Russian newspapers could be diverted, Yaakov Leib did a sterling job selling subscriptions. The wartime censors provided their colleagues in the IB with a list of the names and addresses of people who had taken out subscriptions. The names include those of Yaakov Leib's brother Zalman Kaye (previously Komesaroff, another of my uncles) and his cousin Peter Komesaroff, as well as others who were peripherally linked to the family including B. Pogorelske, the Batagol Brothers, E. Perlman, J. Chanen and S. Brilliant.[24]

A surprising omission from Yaakov Leib's personal file is his very public letter of resignation from the CPA, which was published in the *Australian Jewish News* and *the Australian Jewish Herald* in March 1946.[25] However, the letter is in the ASIO file that records the CPA's interest in the Melbourne Jewish community. The fact the letter is in that file and not in Yaakov Leib's personal file indicates that my uncle's records were most likely culled after he left the Party, or alternatively documents were misplaced when the files were transferred to the newly formed ASIO.

Yaakov Leib's family loved him, especially his siblings for whom he had campaigned (and whom he had financed) to enable them to come to Australia. However, despite their love, they were continually amused by his preparations for the regular meetings of his local branch of the Party, particularly by the way he dressed. Rather than fit in with his working-class comrades, my uncle usually wore a tailored three-piece suit, topped in winter with a double-breasted overcoat trimmed with a fur collar. His outfits seemed more in keeping with a meeting of the local Chamber of Commerce than a gathering of the Communist Party faithful. But then, Yaakov Leib always believed in the importance of personal grooming and presentation.

Yaakov Leib's epiphany that led him to resign from the CPA in 1946 was triggered by his belief that some of his communist confrères would not support an independent Jewish state. In 1946, an Anglo-American Committee of Inquiry was set up to examine conditions in Mandatory Palestine, with a view to recommending future action by the Mandatory power, Britain. The Inquiry took submissions from many sources, including the Communist Party of Great Britain, which was represented by Jack Gaster and Phil Piratin, both sons of prominent British Jews who had been active leaders in the 1936 Battle for Cable Street that resulted in a routing of Oswald Mosley's fascist Blackshirts. These two communist representatives advised the committee that Palestine should become an independent state, with Jews forming a national minority with equal rights. At this time, in 1946, the Holocaust was fresh in people's minds, and most Jews, especially life-long Zionists like my uncle, believed that a sovereign independent Jewish state would be the only protection against another mass murder of Jews. Subsequent events, especially the disintegration of Yugoslavia and Bangladesh's break with Pakistan, demonstrate that artificially created multinational states along the lines recommended by Gaster and Piratin are doomed to failure.

Because of his knowledge of how the Party operated, Yaakov Leib most likely assumed that, in accordance with the Comintern's rules, Gaster and Piratin were articulating the Moscow view which was now opposed to an independent Jewish state.[26] The fact that Gaster and Piratin were Jewish was irrelevant to Yaakov Leib, because, as a secular Jew, he was not as well disposed toward his coreligionists as he was to the religion he practised – communism – so he resigned from the CPA. Initially the Party would not accept Yaakov Leib's resignation and Ralph Gibson, a CPA organiser, came to his house in an attempt to have him reverse his decision. At the time my father (William Komesaroff) was visiting and was asked to leave the room while his brother and Gibson talked, but Gibson's attempts were to no avail, as my uncle was firm in his commitment to abandon the Party. His resignation from the CPA in 1946 shows that Yaakov Leib was far more prescient than many other Party faithful, who waited until the show trials of the 1950s (and beyond) to sever their connection to communism. Also, Yaakov Leib's disillusionment with the Party demonstrates that, for my uncle, Zionism was a far more important ideology than communism.

It is not clear, but I suspect that when he resigned from the Party Yaakov Leib also distanced himself from left-leaning front organisations such as the JCCFA. The National Archives of Australia (NAA) has voluminous files for the Council and I have not found any reference to my uncle in these files for the years after 1946. The files reveal that the Russian newspapers that he had sold and which contributed to the security services' interest in him were handled by another person after 1946.

Yaakov Leib was an occasional contributor to *Letters to the Editor* columns in various newspapers. Mostly he wrote to attack antisemites and their statements, and it is sad that little of this correspondence remains and that none of the letters are included in his file. Yaakov Leib was 26 years of age when he migrated to Australia from Russia so he was not a native English speaker; nonetheless, his letters of protest reveal a confidence and proficiency not normally encountered in foreign-born speakers of English. The first example of his public writings that I found was published in 1919, when he had been in Australia for only five years. The letter, to Peter Simonoff, the Soviet Union's first consul to Australia, refers to the dangers of antisemitism.[27] In the same year he wrote to a contact at *Poale Zion,* a Marxist–Zionist movement in New York, lamenting that Australian Zionists were as hostile to Labour Zionists as 'the American Jewish People are to free [i.e. communist] Russia'.[28]

Many years later, in May 1944, Yaakov Leib wrote to the Burnie (Tasmania) *Advocate* criticising a speech delivered in the Senate by the Tasmanian Labor Senator Richard Darcey. Darcey, a friend of the notorious antisemite Eric Butler, of League of Rights infamy, announced to the Senate that the Jews had started the Russian Revolution. In his letter, Yaakov Leib likened Darcey's thinking to Hitler's accusing the Jews of being communists and at the same time labelling them international capitalists. My uncle ended his polemic by recommending that the Senator read a chapter, 'Jews' Financial Power', in the book *Antisemitism: Historically and Critically Examined*, by the Jewish-Swedish historian Hugo Valentin.[29]

A brief version of Yaakov Leib's letter denouncing Senator Darcey also appeared in the CPA's official newspaper *The Tribune*.[30] This version is not included in Yaakov Leib's file, but it is cited in an immigration file on his younger brother, another of my uncles, Peter Komesarook, who was attempting to sponsor the family of his wife, Rebecca (1903–81), as migrants to Australia. The vetting of sponsors was undertaken by the IB, who also monitored the local communist press. The IB did not recommend the sponsorship because, while they noted that Peter was a 'nice fellow', they did not believe he was financially strong enough to be a suitable guarantor.[31] The fact that the notation is in Peter's and not Yaakov Leib's

Fig. 7: Yaakov Leib Mendelson with his family circa 1925. L to R: Bessie, Minnie, Yaakov Leib and Norman.

file is another indication that, over time, files have been culled.

As with the other Komesaroffs who were the subjects of ASIO surveillance, some of the information recorded in Yaakov Leib's file is clearly incorrect. One entry confuses Yaakov Leib with another person, a much younger man named Mendelsohn [sic], who was born in Poland and arrived in Australia from Manila in 1945. In April 1944 the authorities made a similar mistake, again confusing Yaakov Leib with another person. These errors probably arose because the authorities could not agree on the correct spelling of my uncle's surname, often describing him as 'Mendelsohn' and not 'Mendelson'; his ASIO file is incorrectly labelled 'Mendelsohn'.

Until I began researching, I believed that Yaakov Leib had resigned from the CPA in 1939 in protest over the unexpected and cynical Nazi–Soviet Non-Aggression Pact. By 1939 Hitler's murderous antisemitic policies were well known and I had thought my uncle would have had difficulty in rationalising support for any government aligned with Hitler, especially after the CPA had instructed its members to obstruct what they judged to be Australia's 'imperialist' war effort against Nazi Germany and their Japanese allies. However, Yaakov Leib appears to have continued his Party membership even after June 1940, when Canberra banned the CPA because of concerns that its unswerving allegiance was to the Soviet Union, which was in alliance with Germany, a country Australia was at war with. There was also a fear that because of this alliance Australia could, at some time in the future, find itself at war with the Soviet Union. The ban on the CPA was not removed until December 1942. The fact that Yaakov Leib remained a Party member during this time continues to astonish me. It is possible that he was conflicted initially, and Germany's invasion of the Soviet Union in June 1941 may have resolved his dilemma in favour of the CPA. Another possibility is that he accepted the Party's explanation that Stalin was wisely buying time and diverting Hitler's attention to capitalist countries. It is also possible that he never fully resolved the matter which continued to fester, eventually becoming an element in his 1946 decision to leave the Party.

Yaakov Leib is the only one of the seven people covered in this book who was confirmed to have been a member of the CPA, and I have always had difficulty in understanding the source of his personal, political and religious philosophy. As a youth in Russia he read widely in history and this informed his sophisticated understanding of Zionism, a cause to which he remained committed throughout his life. Yet Yaakov Leib was an avowed atheist who had formed his views well before arriving in Australia. When he was leaving the family home in Grafskoy to start his journey to Australia, his mother, Beila Reeva Komesaroff, had reminded him to follow the Jewish custom of kissing the *mezuzah* at the door when leaving to go on a long journey.[32] In his diary Yaakov Leib records: 'She already knew I did not believe it, and I only did so for her sake'.[33] Yaakov Leib was the only one of the first-generation Komesaroffs in Australia who chose not to observe Jewish law and religious practice. I continually ponder on how and where he developed these views. Because of the restrictions the Russians placed on their Jewish citizens, the family lived in a fairly closed society – not a good environment in which to explore ideas that run counter to those of the community, and in particular those ideas that run counter to the beliefs of one's own family.

While I continue to ponder how Yaakov Leib developed his philosophical views on social and religious questions, they were, nonetheless, not uncommon for East European Jews of his generation and especially for those who, like Yaakov Leib, had migrated from an insular Jewish colony to a more cosmopolitan city. On learning that injustice and antisemitism followed them when they left their closed traditional communities, these Jews became revolutionaries fighting injustice; they believed that only a revolution could bring about much-needed security. As the Jewish philosopher and a leader of the Jewish community in Poland, Stanislaw Krajewski has observed:

> … feelings of hopelessness always lead to radical attitudes. In the case of Jews, lack of hope for satisfactory careers in a society permeated by antisemitism resulted in the belief in the necessity of a revolutionary change of the social order.

It is therefore not surprising that many Jews

welcomed Russia's new Bolshevik government, because they believed that a new order was essential if their lives were to be improved.

In embracing communism, Jewish radicals like Yaakov Leib accepted the premise that in a post-revolutionary society all people would be equal, so there would be no antisemitism. And certainly, during the early years of the republic that was to become the Soviet Union, Jewish life did improve; Jews were free to live and study where and what they wanted. During this initial period, the pogroms that had characterised the Tsarist period seemed to be a thing of the past, and there was a belief that communism had created a utopia that included the Jews. However, this hiatus did not last long. By 1922, when Stalin had become General Secretary of the Communist Party of the Soviet Union's Central Committee, the Jews were again vulnerable, and discrimination became an ever-increasing fact of life for the Jewish population. Unfortunately it took many years before Jewish adherents to communism realised they had been duped. Sadly, in my uncle's case, the realisation came towards the end of his life.

6
Myer Nathan

Myer Nathan was born in Melbourne in 1916. He was the eldest child of Cecilia Nathan (née Komisaruk) who had come to Australia in 1912 to marry David Zmood. However, the marriage ended in divorce in 1928, and some time later Cecilia and her three children (Myer, Tybel and Moses) changed their surname to Nathan, while David changed his surname from Zmood to Davies.[1]

Myer's ASIO file was opened in September 1959 after the Victoria Police Special Branch had traced him as the driver of a car that had been reported at Unity Hall in Bourke Street when a CPA function was held there.[2] Unity Hall was owned by the Australian Railways Union and the talk attended by Myer was delivered by Jimmy Coull, a CPA member and leader of the Liquor Trades Union. The car, owned by Myer's sister Tybel (who did not drive), was reported at the same location in December 1959, and this time the lecture, entitled: 'I saw socialism in practice', was delivered by Ernie O'Sullivan, a member of the CPA who had just returned from a visit to Eastern bloc countries. Myer was again seen driving his sister's car to Unity Hall in January 1960, when another communist, Eric

Thornton, spoke on 'Antisemitism and the Nazi revival'.

The reports of Myer's attendance at CPA meetings and the presence of his sister's car at Unity Hall led ASIO to request the Victorian Special Branch to make enquiries about the Nathans. The officer delegated with this task contacted a friend at the local post office who was unable to help, except that 'he knew Mrs Nathan and did not like her, as she was sour and unfriendly'.[3] Hardly objective counter-intelligence pearls of wisdom! The source made no reference to Myer, nor did the informant seem aware that there was another brother, Moses.

Myer Nathan's file ends abruptly and without explanation at some time after 1960. With the exception of Myer's name and date of birth, the final folio – the last of ten – is fully redacted, the only large-scale redaction in any of the seven files on the Komesaroff family members. For a likely fellow-traveller who attended three CPA lectures over a period of four months, the file is not very large. There is no suggestion in the file that because of his attendance at CPA functions, Myer was a member of the Party. Nonetheless, shortly before his death in 1998, Myer readily admitted to a close relation that as a youth in the 1930s he had joined the CPA and this had been one of the biggest mistakes of his life. He claimed to have resigned in 1968 in protest over the Warsaw Pact's invasion of Czechoslovakia.

As with some other members of his family who have ASIO files, Myer is revealed to be a man with strong – even zealous – pro-Soviet tendencies, who seems to have remained devoted to the communist cause, even when Stalin formed the non-aggression alliance with Hitler and there was ample evidence of state-sponsored anti-semitism in the Soviet Union. This devotion is shown in Myer's contributions to the Letters to the Editor columns of newspapers. For example, towards the end of World War II, Myer wrote to the Melbourne *Age* suggesting that the 'German-Russo' [sic] non-aggression pact was necessary for Russia's defence and that the Soviet Union's unprovoked attack on Finland was a consequence of the Soviet Union being 'obliged to take serious measures to increase its security'.[4] At the time the CPA was articulating the view that 'Finland was a reactionary vassal of imperialism'.[5]

Myer's strong interest in Russia and communism is confirmed by the books in his small library, which were English translations of Russian monographs published in the 1920s and '30s that extolled communism and the Soviet Union. His library was left to a family member after he passed away.

I find it strange that there are no ASIO files on Myer's mother (Cecilia) or his sister (Tybel). In his extensive study of the descendants of the Vilna Gaon, Chaim Freedman notes that for many years Tybel was a member of the CPA and that the house she shared with her mother (Cecilia) was decorated with photographs of Lenin and Trotsky.[6] I have been told that Cecilia brought the pictures from Russia when she left to come to Australia. However, this explanation of the pictures' source is unlikely as Cecilia arrived in Australia in 1912 when Trotsky was relatively unknown and had yet to join the Bolshevik Party.

I have heard reports from other family members and friends who knew both women and they described them as uncritical supporters of communism. There was even a suggestion that the breakdown of Cecilia's marriage was due to her unquestioning loyalty to the communist cause, which was a continual source of conflict with her more politically moderate husband. However, after an extensive search of files that ASIO has made available through the National Archives of Australia (NAA), I was not able to find any reference to Cecilia or to her daughter Tybel. My search included records such as personality profiles of CPA members and Party registers obtained by ASIO's agents, but I found no mention of either of these two women.[7] It is possible that they were fellow travellers and not members of the Party, although my research has shown that ASIO's records are incomplete and, accordingly, the absence of a dossier on or reference to a person does not preclude their Party membership. However, the fact that both women regularly attended synagogue suggests that it is unlikely they were members of the CPA.

ASIO report that they have no record of the third Nathan sibling, Moses, who, during the 1940s, changed his name to John Robert Spencer.[8] None of the surviving family members can recall ever meeting Moses (or John), who passed away in 1980, and family folklore records that he alone among the Nathan siblings was apolitical.

Fig. 8: L to R: Lionel Hart, Motel Zmood and Myer Nathan. Motel and Myer are the sons of David Nathan (also known as Zmood). Myer's mother was Cecilia Nathan, née Komisaruk.

7

Peter Komesaroff

Pinkhas Komisaruk, or Peter Komesaroff, as he was known in Australia, was born in Berdiansk, Ukraine (then part of the Russian Empire; now in Ukraine), in 1898, the fourth surviving child of Meir Komisaruk. Peter came to Australia in 1913 with his siblings and his brother-in-law Zalman Komesaroff (who later changed his name to Kaye). Peter's younger brother, Louis, also merited his own ASIO file.

In 1916 during the Great War, having been in Australia for only three years and despite being below the minimum legal age for enlistment, Peter ran away from Melbourne to New South Wales, falsified his age (he claimed to be 22 years and ten months old) and joined the Australian Army (Australian Imperial Force; AIF). His enlistment papers record his height as 5 feet 3 inches (160 cm) and his chest measurement as 34 inches (83.4 cm).[1] Obviously it was much easier for him to falsify his age than it was to manipulate his physical measurements!

After induction Peter was shipped to the Middle East and then Europe, where he was badly wounded in fighting on the Western Front. Peter received medical attention in England but was not repatriated to Australia until after the end of the war, and the injuries he sustained in fighting for his new country affected his health for the rest of his life.

As the following story testifies, Peter was a very principled man with a strong sense of social justice. During World War II, at a public meeting held in August 1943 by the Carlton-Fitzroy sub-branch of the Returned Soldiers', Sailors' and Airmen's Imperial League of Australia (RSS & AILA), a resolution was put: 'protesting against foreign-born persons and naturalised British subjects being permitted to sell any commodity in the area [...] So-called naturalised aliens were only aliens after all and should be stopped from carrying on business in the district while Australians were away fighting', argued the sub-branch president.[2] Peter, an active RSS & AILA member and an executive of the neighbouring Brunswick sub-branch, was present at this meeting. He stood up and asked if the motion included him, a naturalised British subject who had been crippled serving in the AIF. Despite his opposition, the resolution was carried, after which Peter again stood up, tore off his RSS & AILA badge, tossed it at the chairman of the meeting and announced he was resigning from the League because he believed it to be 'a fascist-controlled organisation'.[3] Interestingly, the meeting had not been endorsed by the Melbourne head office of the RSS & AILA, which subsequently issued a statement that it found the motion repugnant.[4]

His brush with the RSS & AILA would suggest that

Peter should have a voluminous ASIO file dating back many years, but surprisingly the file is remarkably thin – only five folios – and apparently it was opened only in September 1953, when an informer drew ASIO's attention to an advertisement in the *Jewish Herald* for the Commonwealth-sponsored Fellowship of Australian Writers.[5] The advertisement is not included in the file but there is a reference note from ASIO's Regional Director for Victoria which showed the names of people referred to in the advertisement who were known to ASIO. Some of the people listed were known to be communists, some were writers, and some were both. Peter Komesaroff's name is recorded because his phone number appeared in the advertisement. However, in Peter's ASIO file, despite its appearance of being new, the first folio notes that Peter was already known to ASIO through his file (VPF 127) that was started in the 1930s, probably by an ASIO forerunner, the Commonwealth Investigation Branch (CIB). Unfortunately these early papers are no longer available; they were probably destroyed during an earlier document rationalisation, or they were not transferred to ASIO when the organisation replaced the Commonwealth Investigation Service (CIS) as Australia's counter intelligence agency.

It is most likely that Peter first came to the attention of the security services in 1933, when he represented Gezerd (see chapter 4) at a conference organised by the State Provisional Anti-War Committee.[6] His role as foundation Honorary Secretary of the Jewish Council to Combat

Fascism and Anti-Semitism (JCCFA) would also not have passed unnoticed. Apart from his role in the Council, Peter was quick to use the mainstream media to challenge what he saw as antisemitism, and this practice would also have drawn attention to him.[7] There is no suggestion in his file that Peter ever joined the CPA; however, some of his family believe that he was a member, but resigned in the 1950s as knowledge of Stalin's antisemitic brutality became known outside the Soviet Union. It is possible this information is contained in the first part of the file which cannot now be located. However, I doubt that Peter was ever a member of the CPA. As will be explained in chapter 9, in 1940 Inspector Roland Browne, head of the Melbourne office of the CIB, claimed to know Peter and vouched for his loyalty. I find it hard to believe that the inspector would have done this had there been any suggestion that Peter was a communist. Also, a former executive member of the Party who resigned in 1954 knew Peter's children, but cannot recall him (Peter) ever having joined the CPA.

For many years Peter was an active member of the Carlton branch of the ALP, but his membership is another important fact that is not recorded in his ASIO file.

Peter became a naturalised citizen in 1936 and his naturalisation file includes the following comment from the Victorian Special Branch, which was asked to comment on his character and suitability as an Australian citizen: '… he holds advanced views but not incompatible with good citizenship and is not a member of the Communist

Party'.[8] Peter's daughter, Thelma Webberley, believed that her father was a socialist and not a communist, and that possibly Stalin cured him even of being a socialist.[9]

The second entry in Peter's ASIO file, also from an informer, is dated 18 October 1957 and reports on a meeting of the Essendon Branch of the Eureka Youth League – the youth wing of the CPA – where a delegate mentioned that he had been experiencing difficulties with his eyes and had had excellent results from treatment by a local optician, one Peter Komesaroff. Unless communism is infectious, it is hard to understand why such an innocuous comment would have resulted in an entry in an ASIO file.

The next file entry lists subscribers to the Australasian Book Society and includes Peter's name and address. The acquisition of this list also necessitated payment to an informant.

The last entry in the file is a report from an unidentified woman, another informant, who claimed that she had been told by the communist author Judah Waten that Peter was a cousin of Mena Werder, who for a period was married to Felix Werder, the German-born composer who had come to Australia in 1940 on the infamous internee ship HMT *Dunera*. As with much of the information supplied by informers, ASIO probably overpaid for this information, because the informant failed to report that Mena was Waten's sister and the siblings were first cousins of Peter's wife Sarah (née Isaacman). Nowhere in Peter's meagre file is this detail recorded, nor is the fact that in 1942 he was the Consul for the Soviet Union in Victoria.[10] I would have expected that representing a country, the Soviet Union, that had previously been allied with Germany, a country that Australia was at war with, should have attracted the attention of Australia's wartime security service.

Peter's military file includes a letter written in March 1944 by the secretary of the JCCFA to the National War Memorial in Canberra, seeking details of Peter's '... war history, decorations etc.', which were to be used 'in the compilation of a Jewish record of services'.[11] This seems a strange request to have come from the JCCFA and one I have not seen in the service records of others who were members of the Council. More surprising is the fact that the letter did not attract the attention of Australia's security services, and this can possibly be explained by the fact that the Council had only recently been formed. Had the request been made after the formation of ASIO, I believe that a copy of the letter would certainly have been placed in Peter's ASIO file.

During World War II, Peter was active in the formation of the Jewish War Effort Circle (JWEC), of which he was Honorary Secretary. The Circle, which was a response by Australia's Eastern European Jews to a series of antisemitic incidents, worked closely with the Red Cross to provide servicemen and women of all faiths with various comforts. In the first three years of the War the Circle distributed £25,000 to patriotic funds, and provided two cars for the Australian Comfort Funds Appeal and £1,369 to the Heidelberg Military Hospital.[12] The JWEC also supplied prayer books to Jewish servicemen and women, but this and its other charitable activities did not meet with the approval of the old Anglo segment of Australia's Jewish community, who complained the work was unnecessary and would '... do more harm than good in combating Anti-semitism'.[13] Peter responded to this charge by arguing that: 'We as Jews insist on our rights to be protected against Anti-semitism'.[14]

Like his other first-generation cohorts with ASIO files (his cousin Yaakov Leib Mendelson and his brother Louis Komesaroff), Peter was an avid writer of newspaper Letters to the Editor, especially when it came to challenging antisemitism and defending the State of Israel. In 1949, shortly after the creation of Israel, he wrote to the Melbourne *Argus* correcting an article by an anti-communist representative of the pre-war Polish government who had claimed that because of the difficulties it faced, Israel would end up like Poland – occupied by more powerful neighbours. Challenging the analogy, Peter wrote that Israel was different from Poland because '... it is based on truth, justice and democracy and if left alone Jews and Arabs will settle their differences in a matter of weeks'.[15]

In June 1940, during the darkest days of World War II, Peter wrote to the Melbourne *Argus*, challenging a letter from a C. F. Bardwell of Elwood, who had written to the paper objecting to Australia accepting Jewish refugees from Germany because they could not quickly shake off their former allegiances. In a tightly written response, Peter wrote that because they enjoy equality of citizenship, Jews must be loyal to Australia, and he cited the fact that many had enlisted in active service to fight the common enemy – German Nazis, who he described as 'the beasts of civilisation'. Peter concluded his letter by urging Bardwell:

> ... not to waste his energies in antisemitic letters to the Press ... Let Jew and gentile, having the freedom of the world at heart fight shoulder to shoulder in the struggle against the greatest menace the world has ever known.[16]

Peter's tireless work for Jewish causes, particularly in support of his coreligionists fleeing Nazism, is another aspect of his public life that is not revealed in the ASIO file. In the late 1930s Peter personally organised individual members of the Jewish community to sponsor these refugees as migrants to Australia. After the War, Peter was the Victorian Director of Aid for Israel, which today is known as the United Israel Appeal. He was also active in the group that created Australia's first Jewish day school, Mount Scopus College in Melbourne.

The fact that much of Peter's political and communal life is not recorded in his ASIO file is similar to the lack of recording such features in the security service files that were opened on other members of the Komesaroff family, especially his first-generation cohorts – his brother Louis Komesaroff and cousin Yaakov Leib Mendelson. Another common feature of the Komesaroff family files is that the security service officers did not always correctly

Fig. 9: Private Peter Komesaroff, No 1684, Salisbury Plain, England, October 1917.

identify their surveillance target. In February 1944, the Commonwealth Censor intercepted a telegram from 'Komesarook, Pearlman (and) Pogorelski' to the Soviet government in Moscow. The telegram referred to the bulk importation of Russian-language literature that extolled the Soviet war effort. In alerting his head office in Canberra to the interception, The Deputy Director of Security in Victoria reported that the three men, who were related to each other, were well known to the security service and while they '… were pro-Communist and pro-Russian in their sympathy', they were not of interest to the service.[17] At the time, the only Komesarook in Australia was my uncle Peter Komesarook who was serving with the Australian army in northern Victoria and it is unlikely that, at that time, he would have been involved with the Soviet government. However, the telegram most likely refers to his cousin Peter who went by the surname Komesaroff and not Komesarook. Another example of the security service not correctly identifying their target.

8

Louis Komesaroff

Judah Leib Komisaruk, or Louis Komesaroff as he was known in Australia, was the younger brother of Peter Komesaroff (see chapter 8). Louis was born in the port city of Berdiansk on the Black Sea coast of modern-day Ukraine in 1899, the fifth surviving child of Meir Komisaruk. He arrived in Australia as a teenager in 1913.

At 124 pages, Louis' file is the largest of the seven Komesaroff files, but his dossier was unnecessarily bulked up by several reports where investigators confused him with other people, especially his brother Peter and their cousin Yaakov Leib Mendelson, both of whom earned their own ASIO files. Louis' file, the earliest of the seven, was opened in 1918 when the military censor translated a Yiddish-language letter from Kopel Cohen in Russia to one 'Leon Komesdraff' [sic]. Apart from the fact that the spelling of the surname was significantly different, it is doubtful whether the reference was to Louis, as the person named 'Leon' was twelve years older and lived, not in Melbourne where Louis lived, but in Horsham, Victoria.[1] The translated letter mentions 'Leon's' wife, who had passed away, and his child and his sick parents. Louis was not married at that time and both his parents had passed away around 1906 when he was still a young child. 'Leon' was born in the same year as Louis' cousin, my uncle, Yaakov Leib Komesarook (later Mendelson) and many of the details for 'Leon' match those of Yaakov Leib's life, with the exception being that Yaakov Leib's wife was alive at that time. The argument for 'Leon' being Yaakov Leib is strengthened by a handwritten note added later to the file from 'Leon Komesaroff' wishing to change his 'name from Leon Komesaroff to Jacob Leib Komesarook'. A later folio records 'Leon's' date of birth as 16 September 1888, which coincides with my uncle's birth date. With this additional information I am in no doubt that 'Leon' was Yaakov Leib Komesarook and not Yaakov Leib's cousin Yehuda Leib (Louis) Komesaroff. Over the years, because of the similarity of their first names, the security agencies continually confused these two cousins. Indeed, in 1940, the Commonwealth Investigation Branch (CIB) directed its field officers to identify Louis, as they had four files for people with the surname Komesaroff.[2]

The next major entry in Louis' file is in March 1933, when the CIB monitored a business trip he took to Wonthaggi in Victoria. At the time Louis was working as a travelling optician and the officer filing the report wrote that he viewed the 'optical work' as a 'blind' for the great deal of communist work Louis was doing in the district.[3] The officer also noted that Louis was regarded 'as being a dangerous and very subtle individual' who was 'putting in some good work at Wonthaggi on behalf of the C.'s [communists]'.

Fig. 10: Louis Komesaroff and his wife Fanny (née Feinberg) on their wedding day, 25 August 1925.

Despite the adverse report on his activities in Wonthaggi, there was no follow-up on what Louis was doing or why he was in the area. The next entry in his file is in June 1940, when T. J. Edwards of Maffra, Victoria, wrote a letter of complaint about Louis to the Minister of Defence. At the time the CPA had been banned under wartime regulations because of the non-aggression pact between the Soviet Union and Australia's enemy, Germany. Edwards' letter, which is lengthy – more than two typed pages – refers to 'Komesaroff's propaganda' and makes many serious but unsubstantiated allegations about Louis' loyalty. However, it seems that the purpose of the letter was to seek the support of the security agency against legal action threatened by Louis, because Edwards' unfounded public criticism had caused Louis to lose business. Even though the complaint strongly suggested self-interest, it was passed on to the head of the CIB in Canberra, Colonel Harold E. Jones.

Jones asked his office in Melbourne to supply a background note on Louis, and the Melbourne agents provided a very comprehensive briefing that included a detailed medical history. On reading the note, Inspector Roland Browne of the CIB's Melbourne office wrote: 'I would hesitate to call this man a Fifth Columnist' and suggested that a 'warning about careless talk in these difficult times from a person who would command his respect might not be amiss'.[4] The only problem was that the briefing referred, not to Louis, but to his brother Peter. Again the CIB had confused Louis with another person.

Browne was unaware of the mistake, but when the error was brought to his attention, he spoke to Peter about his young brother Louis. As a consequence of this meeting, Louis took the bold step of coming to Melbourne from his home in Bairnsdale to confront the CIB over Edwards' allegations. Louis explained to the interviewing officers that he had regarded Edwards as a friend with whom he frequently discussed international affairs, but the man was also a customer who was behind on his account, and it was possibly for this reason that Edwards had made the allegations against him. In his note of the meeting, Inspector Browne describes Louis as 'of Russian Jewish birth (who) has assertive qualities in argument'. He also mentions that in recent times Louis had formed a group to assist soldiers' dependants. The note, dated 16 August 1940, concludes with the following sentence: 'I have known the Komesaroffs for years – there are several serving in the war. I have no doubt about their basic loyalty although they are somewhat "leftist" in their views'.[5]

Prior to joining the CIB as head of its Melbourne operation, Browne had been a major in military intelligence and it was probably in his role as an army officer that he had come in contact with the Komesaroff family, especially Peter, who, in 1916 had falsified his age so he could join the Australian Imperial Force (AIF). Peter's enlistment would have appealed to Browne, who thought that a true test of a person's right to Australian citizenship was a willingness to join the armed services, particularly during a time of war. Despite linking military service to citizenship, Browne was seen as 'an enlightened liberal' who 'exercised common sense'. He strongly defended anti-Nazi Jewish immigrants and was not predisposed to sentence left-wing migrants to internment.[6] Judging by a handwritten notation at the foot of a letter to Browne written by Israel Sher, of the Jewish Council to Combat Fascism and Anti-Semitism (JCCFA), it appears that Browne was on reasonably civil terms with the subjects of his investigations. At the end of the official letter, which was on the Council's letterhead, Sher, who was not a member of the Party, wrote: 'My personal and kind regards to yourself and Mrs Browne' – a note that suggests the two men and their wives had met socially.[7]

Browne's endorsement of the Komesaroff family did not lead to the closure of Louis' file, because within months of his report an unsigned letter turned up at the censor's office claiming that Louis and his family, as well as his wife's family, were communists who were disloyal to Australia and refused to stand during the playing of the national anthem.[8] The unknown writer urged the police to watch Louis because he was doing harm to the country. The authorities appear to have ignored this letter, but a note from the Bairnsdale police in 1949 drew attention to Louis' pro-Russian views and asserted that as president of the local branch of the Australian Labor Party (ALP), he had stacked the branch with radicals. The policeman wrote that he believed that Louis was 'a keen and enthusiastic supporter of Communism' who was 'a strong, silent shrewd worker in the cause of Communism', even though, as the officer readily admitted, there was 'insufficient proof of this'.[9]

The file shows no follow-up action after this note, with the next folio dated more than eighteen months later, reporting that communist activity had fallen in Bairnsdale since Louis had gone to live in Melbourne. Learning that Louis had come to their area, police from the Special Branch in Melbourne took another look at him, but 'failed to discover any activity by him … for the last two years'.

One of the last file entries, in May 1967, was the consequence of an intercepted telephone call between Louis and the Australia-Soviet Friendship Society Tourist Group. Louis had initiated the call as he was planning an overseas business trip and wanted to include the Soviet Union on his itinerary. Three years earlier, in February 1964, Louis had written to the CIB explaining the reasons he and his wife wished to visit the Soviet Union and Czechoslovakia – 'the same reasons [sic] which applies to all the other countries which we wish to visit, namely to see all these countries for ourselves'. The file does not reveal the reason for the letter, but most likely Louis was seeking to have his Australian passport approved for travel to the Soviet Union. Unfortunately Louis passed away before he could make his longed-for visit to the USSR.

Apart from a surveillance report from an informant noting that in July 1963 Louis had attended a reception for the Georgian State Dancers (which had been hosted by the Australia-Soviet Friendship Society), and a copy of a letter Louis had written to the Melbourne *Jewish News* in support of the JCCFA, the rest of Louis' file consists of extensive extracts from the file on his son, Max, and a couple of folios reporting on his daughter, Tessa. These extracts report that the father (Louis) had made, 'in the past, very assertive statements of a pro-Russian variety and anti-British statements. He could be classified as a suspected communist'.[10] This statement was made despite earlier investigations concluding that there was insufficient proof that Louis was a communist, and despite Inspector Browne's belief that although Louis was a supporter of the left, he had no doubt about his loyalty.

Details of Max's and Tessa's files are discussed in the next two chapters.

Like his elder brother Peter, Louis was an early member of the JCCFA, but, surprisingly, ASIO has no record of his membership and, apart from a copy of Louis' letter to the Melbourne *Jewish News* supporting the JCCFA, it appears that ASIO was unaware of his association with the Council. The letter was written shortly before the Council was expelled from the Victorian Jewish Board of Deputies (VJBD), and in it Louis argues in support of the Council and its officials.[11] He refers to his many years living in Gippsland where he had ample evidence of the Council's excellent work on behalf of the Jewish community.

Another surprise, particularly given the criticism of him by some people in Bairnsdale, is that the file does not contain any of the many letters and articles Louis wrote for publication in the local press, particularly the

Gippsland Times.¹² Examination of contemporary newspapers reveals Louis to have been a prolific writer and campaigner on three issues: support for Russia against Germany, support for a Jewish homeland and opposition to antisemitism. Louis' writing seems to have dropped off during the period when Germany and Russia had a non-aggression pact and the Party was banned in Australia, but picked up in late 1942 when the Curtin government lifted the ban.

When Louis became aware of the extent of Stalin's great purges, it is believed that he wrote to Stalin seeking his confirmation that the country's Jews were not being persecuted. Louis' family understand that he received a response to his letter from the Soviet Foreign Minister, Vyacheslav Molotov, who, understandably, wrote denying that the Soviet Union was oppressing its Jewish citizens and pointing out that antisemitism was illegal in his country.¹³ I have not been able to locate the letter, nor I have been able to independently verify if and when the correspondence occurred, but if it is true then it is somewhat ironic, as Molotov's wife, who was Jewish, was arrested in 1949, charged with being a Zionist and sent into internal exile, where she remained until 1953, when Stalin died and she re-married Molotov. Louis' correspondence with the Soviet leadership suggests a naivety that could be explained by his disillusionment with the Soviet system. Like most other Jews who believed that the Soviets had created a utopia that had emancipated its Jewish citizens, he could now see that, despite the rhetoric, in the Soviet

Union communism had not eliminated the persecution of Jews. In this he did not diverge from the views of many of his close relations and coreligionists who had once perceived the Soviet Union as a utopia for Jews, but now saw that the Soviets had betrayed this dream and were now persecuting its Jewish citizens.

Louis' letters to the press reveal a proud Jew and a passionate Zionist who had a strong interest in international affairs and was remarkably perceptive. He was driven by his antipathy towards antisemitism, which he linked with fascism. Until he became aware of Soviet antisemitism, Louis' positive, almost idealistic attitude to Russia was another factor that shaped his thinking. All these characteristics are revealed in the following extract from a letter, to the Melbourne *Argus*, which he wrote in 1940 when communism was temporarily banned in Australia and Russia had a non-aggression pact with Germany:

> Russia should be reminded that arming herself in isolation from the rest of the world will not stop the Germans from plundering one country after another until it precipitates war on a world wide scale, including Russia. You will say that Germany has a non-aggression pact with Russia. What are Hitler's pacts worth? Hitler the liar has broken more than he can remember.[14]

Given subsequent events, these sentiments were remarkably prescient.

Fig. 11: Louis Komesaroff.

9

Max Komesaroff

Of the seven files released by ASIO, none is more egregious than that of Max Komesaroff.[1] Max, Louis Komesaroff's son, was born in Melbourne in 1927 and, like many of the second-generation Komesaroffs born in Australia, he distinguished himself academically, earning a residential scholarship to Ormond College at the University of Melbourne, where he graduated first as Bachelor of Optometry – following in the footsteps of his father – and later as Bachelor of Geophysics. For most of his working life, Max was involved with the radio telescope at Parkes in western New South Wales, and much of his published research is still cited in academic journals.[2]

Max appears to have come to ASIO's attention because, like his father Louis, he was a member of the Jewish Council to Combat Fascism and Anti-Semitism (JCCFA). It was as a representative of that organisation that he visited the Attorney-General of Victoria, Trevor Oldham, in 1949, to protest a proposal by the State Liberal Government to amend the Police Offences Act to make it an offence to: 'excite abhorrence against any religion or religious denomination or sect or against any members of any religious denomination or sect'.[3] Those found guilty of the offence were liable to a fine of £100 or twelve months in gaol.[4] The proposed amendments bring to mind the current controversy surrounding Section 18C of the *Racial Discrimination Act* 1975 (regarding offensive behaviour because of race, colour or national or ethnic origin), except that the 1949 proposal was strongly opposed by the left side of politics, particularly by CPA members and fellow travellers while today it is the right that want to abolish 18C because they claim it constrains free speech.

Initially Oldham claimed the proposed amendments were designed to punish those disseminating extreme anti-Catholic or antisemitic propaganda, but when pressed he changed his tune and agreed that the amendments were directed against the CPA, 'which was fostering dissension among religious groups in an attempt to further its own policy'.[5]

Known as the Anti-Bigotry Bill, the proposal was, as expected, roundly condemned by the mainstream press, but the greatest and most vocal opposition came from the union movement, especially those on the left or under the control of the CPA. On the other hand, the legislation was strongly supported by the Catholic Church and in particular by its influential Melbourne leader, Archbishop Daniel Mannix. The Sydney *Sunday Herald* summed up the view of civil libertarians when it said: 'How convenient it is becoming to defend any illiberal or repressive proposal by declaring it anti-Communist in purpose! …

Because Communists and fellow travellers are against it, everyone else is expected to be for it.'[6]

The JCCFA opposed the Anti-Bigotry Bill because it believed that the Bill violated civil liberties and would prevent Jews from criticising antisemitic religious denominations.[7] However, in his 1968 study of the Council's structure and function, Allan Leibler claims that the true motive for the Council's opposition was that the proposed legislation would have silenced communist criticism of the Catholic Church.[8] I believe that both these explanations are applicable in that the Bill would have protected religious groups that advanced anti-Jewish arguments and the communists would have had to abandon their attacks on anti-communist church groups.

After receiving numerous delegations seeking the withdrawal of the Bill, the government abandoned the planned changes and, although the matter was forgotten by many, including the protesters, ASIO was busy assembling files on the 'communists and fellow travellers' who had opposed the legislation. Included in this group was Max Komesaroff. An entry in his file, dated 11 May 1951, refers to a report in the Melbourne *Herald* of 23 September 1949, which listed the names of organisations whose representatives had visited the Attorney-General to request him to withdraw the proposed legislation. The newspaper report explicitly stated that the protesters were communists and mentioned one 'M. Komesaroff who represented the Jewish Council to Combat War and Fascism [sic]'.[9]

The file note – written nearly two years after the newspaper report referring to Max – states that a search of ASIO records 'had failed to reveal any further trace of M. Komesaroff being associated with any of the Jewish societies on record', so the investigating officer concluded that the 'M. Komesaroff' was Max Komesaroff. Later in the file, mention is made that the 'M. Komesaroff' referred to in the report may not have been Max, and later still there is a hand-written notation stating: 'Identification is unsatisfactory'.[10] Despite the file notation that the identification needed to be confirmed, there is no record showing that this was ever done, or that 'M. Komesaroff' could have been someone other than Max. The lack of source validation is a continuing theme in the seven ASIO files on the Komesaroff family.

The possibility that 'M. Komesaroff' could have been Max's cousin, Morris Komesaroff, did not seem to be a concern. Morris (see chapter 13 for details of his file) was six years older than Max and in his later life he had numerous confrontations with the authorities over civil liberties. However, Morris' son believes that it is unlikely that the 'M. Komesaroff' referred to in Max's file was his father.

Max's case (and reputation) was not helped by the fact that the newspaper report that erroneously named him a communist also linked him to Brian Fitzpatrick, who was well known to ASIO as a troublesome fellow-traveller who was secretary of the Australian Council of Civil Liberties which the CPA boasted was under its control.[11]

Early in Max's ASIO file an officer reported that he 'is the son of Judah Leib [Louis] Komesaroff about whom there is a considerable file consisting of allegations regarding communist sympathies'.[12] However, the officer did acknowledge that despite investigation, the allegations were never substantiated.

As a geophysicist working with the Bureau of Mineral Resources (BMR), Max required a security clearance for his daily work, so ASIO's interest in him would now follow him for the rest of his working life. This, despite his colleagues and supervisors reporting that Max was 'a quiet, unobtrusive and a satisfactory worker', who was not 'revealed as anything but a hard-working person'. Ultimately ASIO's head office concluded that Max was an unlikely security risk and directed its Victorian Regional Director to advise the Public Service Inspector that there was no adverse report against him. 'However, his name should be kept in mind by Victorian Officers who deal with CSIRO [Commonwealth Scientific, Industrial and Research Organisation] or the University'.[13]

In June 1953 a requirement for Max to visit the Northern Territory to work with the BMR's Airborne Scintillometer Unit prompted ASIO to have another look at Max and his father. On this occasion the Victorian Special Branch was asked to investigate both men to see if they harboured any sympathy for Russia, the CPA or any allied front organisation, with particular attention to the JCCFA. The Special Branch constable delegated to make the enquiries consulted the local electoral roll

Fig. 12: Max Komesaroff who graduated in both physics and optometry from the University of Melbourne.

before approaching neighbours, who reported that the Komesaroff family kept to themselves but were known to have parties where people spoke in foreign languages. The informant added that the family had a good reputation, although he considered Louis to be 'ill mannered'. The informant judged Max to be 'unlike a normal youth in such [sic] that he has a habit of walking with his head down. He does not seem to have the normal interests of a man of his age and lacks the spring in his step'.[14] Clearly very subjective and irrelevant observations!

Nothing came of the Victorian Special Branch's investigation, because before it was completed Max had resigned from the BMR to join the Division of Radiophysics of the CSIRO in Sydney, and the Victorian file was passed to ASIO's NSW office. The file is surprising because it does not include any record of the work that ASIO's NSW agents would have undertaken in clearing Max to take up his appointment with the CSIRO. At the time of Max's transfer, in 1953, a period of anti-communist hysteria still prevailed, and suspected communists and their sympathisers were being removed from sensitive organisations such as the CSIRO. While Max was certainly no communist, he was joining an organisation that had lost several prominent people because of a campaign for the tighter screening of scientists who were seeking to join research establishments such as the CSIRO or who were working on projects that had a security content.[15] A few years before Max joined the CSIRO Division of Radiophysics, the Division had lost a leading member, Thomas Kaiser, because he was a communist, and his continued political activity had made it necessary for him to leave Australia permanently.[16]

The file on Max that ASIO's Victorian office transferred to their NSW colleagues included a note that recent articles in the *Jewish Herald* had reported that, in 1947, Max and his sister, Tessa, were well known leaders of the Jewish Students' Group; there was also a note, dated March 1955, that Max was coming to Melbourne to attend a farewell party for Tessa, who was about to leave on an overseas trip to Europe and Israel. No conclusions were drawn and no comments were made about the Jewish Students' Group, which was a group of tertiary students and recent graduates who met to discuss an eclectic range of Jewish topics. The Group was formed in 1941 by Dr David Tabor, a prominent British physicist, who was then undertaking research at the University of Melbourne. Tabor's hope was that the Group would encourage support for Zionism and produce the next generation of leaders for the local Jewish community.[17] Dr Tabor was relatively conservative, although the Group was known to have included left-leaning Jewish students, some of whom were members of the CPA. However, there is no evidence that either Max or his sister had 'graduated' from the Group to the CPA.[18]

The last entry in Max's file is dated October 1969. Marked 'Secret', the folio contains a list of people whose residential addresses appeared in a document obtained from the CPA office in Sydney – presumably acquired in a clandestine raid. But the address given for Max is that of his parents' home in Melbourne – somewhere he had not lived since his move to Sydney fifteen years previously.

There is no evidence to show that, after moving to Sydney, Max continued his membership of the JCCFA; it is more than likely he had severed his connection around 1952, when the Council was expelled from the VJBD. Max's father (Louis) and uncle (Peter), who were at various times on the JCCFA's executive, are understood to have resigned around that time. Despite leaving the Council, Max never forgot his principles, leavened with humour, as demonstrated in the following letter he wrote to the *Sydney Morning Herald* in 1987 following a report that a Queensland businessman, Michael Gore, had referred to visitors from the southern states as cockroaches:

> SIR: Reading the recent comments by Mr Michael Gore on the subject of cockroaches which said, inter alia, 'the streets these days are full of cockroaches and most of them are human', I was reminded of a story told by my Russian Jewish grand-father.
>
> A Jew was selling spectacles in a Prussian town. A Prussian officer seized a pair of spectacles, put them on and then, looking at the Jew, said: 'These spectacles are no good, Jew. When I look through them, all I see is a swine.' The Jew said: 'But that's impossible, these are excellent spectacles.'
>
> The officer repeated his comment and the Jew repeated his protest.

The Jew then seized the spectacles, put them on his own nose, and looking at the officer, said: 'My God, you're right.'

Max Komesaroff [19]

Aside from being a record of the scandalous manner in which he was treated by ASIO and other agencies, Max's file exhibits many characteristics that are also seen in the files on the six other members of the Komesaroff family who came to ASIO's attention – the confused identity that is deemed unsatisfactory, and the gratuitous and irrelevant observations made by neighbours. When Max was deemed not be a security threat, irrelevant information continued to be added to the dossier, such as the information on his planned visit to Melbourne to attend the farewell for his sister. Finally, there is the out-of-date address and the outrageous accusation that he was a communist.

10

Tessa Silberberg

Tessa Silberberg (née Komesaroff), who was born in Melbourne in 1929, has the distinction of being the only woman among the seven Komesaroff family members to have an ASIO file; she is also the third member of her immediate family to have such a file.[1] As noted in chapter 9, her father Louis has an extensive file, as does her brother Max (chapter 9). Tessa's file was opened in October 1954, when an informant provided ASIO with a list of the names and addresses of people who owed money to the Australasian Book Society.[2] In his history of the CPA, Alastair Davidson describes the Australasian Book Society as a communist front organisation.[3] The Society, created in 1952 by a group of mainly CPA members, published cheap editions of books by Australian authors and sold the books to readers who made a commitment to purchase six books per year, for a total cost of fifty shillings ($5). The authors were almost all left-wing with many being Party members. In the first ten years of its existence, the Society published 35 books with an average print run of 4,500 copies. Over time, ASIO devoted an increasing proportion of its resources to monitoring

Australian authors and their readers. As a result of a directive from Prime Minister Robert Menzies in 1952, writers who applied for grants from the then Commonwealth Literary Fund were investigated by ASIO, and communists and their sympathisers were discreetly bypassed for any assistance.

Learning of ASIO's interest in the Australasian Book Society reminded me of visits I had made in the 1980s to remote Siberian (USSR) aluminium smelters. The visits, which were related to my employment with an Australian mining company, were undertaken before the collapse of the Soviet Union, and on each occasion the plant's management would take me to their community library where I was shown the cultural services they provided for their workers. I would always seek out the books by Australian authors; I was never disappointed, as I was usually shown Russian editions of books written by communist authors such as Judah Waten, Frank Hardy and Katharine Susannah Prichard – writers who were popular with the Society's subscribers. At one plant, the local high school was using a translated edition of Alan Marshall's classic *I Can Jump Puddles* as a study text. Marshall, although not a communist, was another author favoured by the Society.

Tessa's passion for literature was not confined to the Australasian Book Society, as she took an interest in a wide range of cultural and political activities. In the 1950s she was friendly with Tim Burstall, a key figure in Australia's post-war film industry, who is probably best known as the director, writer and producer of the raunchy movie *Alvin Purple* and its sequel *Alvin Rides Again*. In his diary, *Memoirs of a Young Bastard*, Burstall mentions Tessa and her brother Max attending one of his parties.[4]

Brief details of Tessa's father (Louis) and brother (Max) are included in her file, as are details of her passport, collected when she applied for travel documents to visit Europe and Israel in 1955.

A later folio reports that Tessa had left Australia on the liner *Stratheden* for an extended trip to England, the Continent and Israel. This important piece of strategic intelligence was sourced from the *Jewish Herald* of 26 November 1954: appropriately, ASIO has tagged the entry 'Secret'.

The last folio in Tessa's file (dated June 1959) is a note reporting on an index book listing the names and addresses of people who had purchased publications from the CPA-owned Pioneer Bookshop in Sydney. Like the first folio in Tessa's file, this information was provided by an informant, who appears to have been very close to the CPA's Sydney branch hierarchy.

Apart from the comment that she was a reader of left-wing literature, no other allegations were made against Tessa, and there are no entries in her file after June 1959. However, Tessa's name does appear in the file of a fellow student and friend, Bernard Rechter, a self-declared member of the CPA until 1954, when he became disillusioned and left the Party.[5] A folio in Bernard's file refers to his involvement with the Melbourne Jewish Youth

Council (MJYC), of which Tessa is recorded as vice-president.[6] The Council seems to have been an alliance of various religious and Zionist youth groups, including the Melbourne Jewish Students' Group. The Council first came to the attention of the Commonwealth Investigation Service (CIS) in 1944 when Council members wrote to the Jewish anti-Fascist Committee (JAFC) in Moscow. The Council was again subject to the attention of CIS in 1946 when the Service believed, incorrectly, that the MJYC had sought affiliation with the World Federation of Democratic Youth, a communist front organisation. The next year, 1947, the MJYC was invited to send a delegate to the Jewish Council to Combat Fascism and Anti-Semitism (JCCFA).

As well as being active in the leadership of the MJYC and the Melbourne Jewish Students' Group, Tessa was a delegate to the National Union of Australian University Students (NUAUS, now known as the Australian Union of Students) and a member of the Melbourne University Labor Club who participated in marches and demonstrations, particularly in relation to the peace movement; however none of this information is recorded in her ASIO file. ASIO also maintained several files on the Melbourne University Labor Club. One of the files covers the period 1947 to 1949, a time when Tessa attended the University of Melbourne to study optometry, and ASIO estimated the Club had around 100 members of whom 25 were suspected of being associated with the CPA. The file lists the 25 Party members and Tessa Komesaroff's name is not

Fig. 13: Tessa Silberberg (née Komesaroff) with her family. (L to R) Fanny Komesaroff (mother), Tessa, Louis Komesaroff (father), Ruth Komesaroff (sister), 25 June 1953.

included.[7] A member of both the Labor Club and the Party whose name appears on ASIO's list has confirmed that Tessa was an active member of the Club, but that she had no connection with the CPA and was probably unaware of how Party members manipulated the Club's activities. As with most front groups, the communist members of the Labor Club worked as a disciplined group, preparing their tactics before each meeting so their motions were seldom rejected.[8]

Tessa suspected, but did not know, that her extracurricular political activities while at university had attracted ASIO's attention. Because of her suspicions, she discussed this with her daughter and, in explaining her youthful political views, Tessa described herself as a 'fellow-traveller'. This is a term with a Russian background used to describe someone who does not accept all the aims of the Communist Party, but is philosophically sympathetic to the Party's economic, social and political goals. Some of Tessa's friends from university were CPA members and, while they readily acknowledge the similarities in their political sympathies, they are adamant that Tessa was never a member of the Party.

11
Morris Komesaroff

The most recent Komesaroff file opened by ASIO is the one for Morris Komesaroff, who was born in Melbourne in 1922. Morris, also known as Moishe, was the eldest son of Alter Komesaroff, who had come to Australia in 1912 and was an older brother of Peter and Louis Komesaroff. A brilliant student, Morris won a competitive scholarship to Scotch College, Melbourne, where he graduated as joint dux in 1939, and was awarded a scholarship to study Law and Arts at the University of Melbourne. After graduating from university Morris had an outstanding legal career specialising in property law; he conceived and developed the strata title form of building subdivision, which revolutionised apartment ownership and remains the legal basis of much of Australia's current residential development.[1]

Morris could be an irritant to officialdom, especially on matters of principle, where he was a fearless and uncompromising advocate. It was through his actions that the Victorian Legal Profession Guarantee Fund was established to compensate clients who suffered losses in their dealings with lawyers. He also persuaded banks to

Fig. 14: Morris Komesaroff, a graduate in law from the University of Melbourne.

pay the interest earned on solicitors' trust accounts into the Fund.

While he could be difficult, even litigious, Morris was never affiliated with any political party, so it is surprising that ASIO took an interest in him.[2] Morris' file was opened in June 1973, when he planned to visit China with his wife and daughter.[3] Gough Whitlam had been elected Prime Minister on 5 December 1972, and on 21 December of that year the new government recognised the communist People's Republic of China (PRC). The previous Australian government had refused to acknowledge the PRC; instead, it had recognised the Republic of China, governed by the Chinese Nationalists on the island of Taiwan, and it was illegal for holders of an Australian passport to travel to the PRC and other communist countries. With the change in recognition, Australian citizens were now permitted to visit mainland China, but the file on Morris suggests that ASIO had yet to modify its practice of recording the details of Australians planning to travel to that country. Newspaper reports of the time show that this was not the only policy of the new government that ASIO had issues with. ASIO opposed the new Prime Minister's decision not to have the organisation provide security clearances for his personal staff, and ASIO also had difficulty with Whitlam's decisions to withdraw Australian troops from Vietnam, to terminate conscription and to grant immediate independence to Papua New Guinea.[4]

For Morris, the visit to China had less to do with politics and more to do with the fact that, with the change in government policy, he and his family could now easily visit an overseas location of interest that had, for many years, been off-limits to Australian citizens.

Morris' file is very slim – only three folios – and contains a list of the names of people who had registered an interest in travelling to China now that it was open to holders of Australian passports. The file note is marked 'Secret' and 'Non Gratis', suggesting that ASIO had paid for the information, which most likely came from an employee of the travel agency that was organising the trip. It is also possible that the informant was affiliated with the CPA, as there is a notation alongside one name in the file that the person was rejected as a potential visitor to the PRC 'on instructions from the Communist Party Australia (Marxist-Leninist)'.[5]

A week after the file was opened, ASIO's informant updated the list of names, which now showed that the China Australia Society, which was organising the trip, had rejected Morris, his wife and daughter as potential visitors to China. The report of the rejection is included in a lengthy memo on the Victorian Branch of the Australia China Society that was written by an ASIO agent. Apart from the list of names of accepted and rejected potential tourists, the memo surveys the Society's pricing strategy and notes that participants could be expected to pay $970 for the fully escorted tour. However, a large portion of the first page of the memo is redacted and it is possible that this blacked-out section could show the reasons for the rejection of the Komesaroff group as potential tourists to China. Alongside the names of the three Komesaroff applicants there is a typed notation 'VPF 22544' and a handwritten jotting '2 Refs', which I interpreted to mean that ASIO possibly has another file that it has not been able to locate.

Despite the initial rejection, Morris and his wife did

travel to China in late 1973. However, their son Paul had made a visit a few months earlier and there is no reference to that trip in Morris' file, nor are there any references to Paul's involvement in anti-Vietnam War protests and other left-wing activities. As was seen with Louis Komesaroff's file, referring to the activities of immediate family members who were of interest to ASIO was a common practice, and the fact this was not done with Morris' file suggests either an error on the organisation's part or else that Paul did not have a file – something he believes is unlikely. It is also possible that any file on Paul would still fall under ASIO's open-access period restrictions.

Morris' file, which is linked to a similar document created for his wife, Hadassah (née Sher), fails to mention her impeccable left-wing credentials. Though not a communist, her father, Israel Sher, had been the inaugural vice-president and later president of the Jewish Council to Combat Fascism and Anti-Semitism (JCCFA) and other Jewish communal organisations that were monitored by ASIO. He was one of the first of the JCCFA's leadership to acknowledge that the Council had been wrong in its stance toward Soviet antisemitism.[6] Hadassah's aunt, Fredda Brilliant, was a sculptor who worked for the Comintern in Moscow during World War II, and her cousins, Rivka Brilliant and Miriam Brilliant, were members of the CPA. ASIO maintained files on all three of these women.

Supporting the view that there were lacunae in ASIO's system is the fact that earlier, in 1966 at the beginning of the Chinese Cultural Revolution, Morris had travelled to

China through Hong Kong without the approval of the Australian government. At the time, Australian passports were marked 'not valid for China or North Vietnam', and violating these restrictions should have attracted ASIO's attention.

12

Michael Komesaroff

I (Michael Komesaroff) am the grandson of Menachem Mendel Komisaruk and the son of William Komesaroff. William was born in Grafskoy in 1908 and came to Australia in 1922. I was born in Melbourne in 1945, the second youngest of the 44 first and second generation of my family who are the focus of this book.

In my youth I was very active in student politics. From 1964 to 1966 I was editor of *Catalyst*, the student newspaper at the Royal Melbourne Institute of Technology (RMIT; now RMIT University), where I campaigned against Australia's involvement in the Vietnam war and in support of other causes, including the 1965 students' New South Wales 'freedom ride' in support of Aboriginal rights. I was also President of the RMIT Labor Club, a member of the Students' Representative Council and a delegate to the National Union of Australian University Students (NUAUS, now known as Australian Union of Students), an organisation that was said to be heavily infiltrated by ASIO. As a result of my student activities I was known to the Victorian police who interviewed me in 1965 after returning from an NUAUS conference in Perth. The interview was a consequence of an article published in *Catalyst* which suggested I was selling copies of *The Group* by the American author Mary McCarthy.[1] At the time the novel was available in Perth but banned in Victoria as it was judged to be offensive to public morals.

Because of my opposition to the Vietnam War, I occasionally spoke on the telephone with Dr Jim Cairns, a left-wing Australian Labor Party member of parliament. Cairns, who was deputy Prime Minister from 1974 to 1975, was the subject of extensive surveillance – he claimed his phone was monitored – so ASIO was most likely aware of our conversations and my left-leaning political philosophy.[2]

Despite my 'radical' youth, I was surprised to learn that ASIO had concluded that I had not satisfied the criteria for them to have established a file on my student activities, especially as this was a period when ASIO was at its most influential and was deploying the greater part of its resources for monitoring dissent within the nation's institutions of higher learning. My surprise turned to shock when, on searching further, I found that there was no record of my frequent business trips (undertaken between 1981 and 1994) to the former Soviet Union and the communist countries of eastern and central Europe. Also, there were no references to my occasional visits to Canberra in the 1980s, when I dined with Yevgeny Samoteykin – the Soviet Union's affable ambassador to Australia from 1983 to 1990 – at his diplomatic residence. Given that ASIO's analysts regarded the Soviet Embassy as having primarily an intelligence function rather than a diplomatic purpose, and given that they estimated that half to two-thirds of the Embassy's personnel were employees of the Soviet security services, I was amazed that my activities were not recorded, all the more so, given that the trade and commercial counsellors with whom I dealt were singled out by ASIO for special scrutiny.[3] My amazement turned to astonishment when I learnt that it was routine ASIO practice to debrief any Australian businessman returning from Moscow.[4] Apart from the incident mentioned in the next paragraph, despite many trips to the Soviet Union, I was never approached by ASIO.

For most of my working life I was employed in the mining industry, and in this capacity I regularly visited communist countries; for a time I lived in Vladivostok, in Russia's Far East, and in Beijing, China. My first visit to the USSR was in 1981 and my last was around 1994, when the USSR no longer existed and Boris Yeltsin, the first President of the Russian Federation, had replaced Mikhail Gorbachev as the country's leader. My work in the Soviet Union was public knowledge with the Australian press reporting on my activities.[5]

My first visit to China was shortly after the Tiananmen Square protests of 1989 and my last was as recently as October 2017. I have travelled widely through both countries, usually as a guest of their respective Ministries for Non-Ferrous Metallurgy. Despite my sustained travels over three and a half decades to such 'suspect' countries, ASIO has no direct record of Michael Benjamin Komesaroff. However, an ASIO agent did visit me in the mid-1980s at my office in Brisbane. The meeting was initiated by the agent, who wanted to learn of my dealings with Soviet officials. I cannot recall the agent's name, but I remember the visit, which was fairly brief as I was conscious of not wanting to offer any encouragement that could lead to further contact with ASIO. My reaction was a considered one, and was largely influenced by the possible consequences should the Soviets learn of my cooperation. I was particularly fearful of some retaliation occurring when I was visiting the USSR.

While I cannot boast of having an ASIO file, I strongly suspect that the Soviet Committee for State Security (KGB) opened a file on me because of an incident that occurred during one of my earliest business trips to Moscow. The incident arose because of events related to my cousin, Ben Sherr, who – apart from me – is the only member of the group of 44 family members to have visited the Soviet Union. Ben, the son of my aunt Yoheved Sherr (née Komisaruk), was born in Grafskoy in 1921 and the following year he migrated to Australia with his parents. After a 1981 meeting in Melbourne with a Russian migrant who carried a message from Miron Faynerman (1953–), Ben decided to visit the Soviet Union. Miron's widowed grandmother (Rivka Faynerman, née Kalikhman) had married Mark (Motel) Komisaruk, my father's first cousin and the grandson of Pinkhas Komisaruk. After the Russian Revolution, Mark was also known as Mark Solomonovich.

Ben's visit to the Soviet Union in 1982 went well, and he and his wife, Miriam, visited Tashkent (in Uzbekistan) where they met Miron, whose family had been evacuated there during World War II. From Tashkent, Miron, Ben and Miriam flew to Yerevan (in Armenia), where Miron worked as a chemical engineer.

Some years later, in July 1986, when Ben learnt that I would be travelling to Moscow, he passed on Miron's contact details and asked that I meet with him while in the Soviet Union. I could not meet with Miron because he lived in Yerevan, but Miron's younger brother, Joseph (1961–), was in Moscow and I had a contact for him through a woman called Esther Tukachinsky. When I landed in Moscow, I contacted Esther, whose son had recently been allowed to leave the country to live in Israel. Esther took me to meet Joseph, a chemist who had worked in a cement factory, but was now unemployed. He was married to Nataly and lived with Nataly's family, Vladimir and Frada Melamed. Over a period of a week I met several times with Esther and Joseph, as well as with Nataly and her family. After one meeting Esther lamented Joseph's 'sad situation'. When I queried her on what she meant, she replied, 'Don't you know? Joseph and his family are *refuseniks*.' I knew well that a *refusenik* was an unofficial term for those individuals, typically but not exclusively Jews, who were denied permission to emigrate from the Soviet Union, and I knew that such people were closely monitored and harassed by the Soviet authorities.

However, a shiver swept through me when I heard the term applied to people I had been in regular contact with. What did consorting with these dissidents mean for me? Would I be rounded up and tossed in gaol for violating Soviet laws?

My fears only increased when I later learnt that Nataly's father, Vladimir Melamed, was a prominent mathematician, but when he applied to leave the Soviet Union for Israel, he had been stripped of his advanced degrees and dismissed from Moscow University, despite having taught there for over 30 years. His apartment was under regular surveillance by the KGB, who confiscated his mail and intercepted his telephone calls. As Vladimir Melamed was under such close attention, it was almost certain that the authorities would have reported on my visit to his apartment and my meetings with his daughter and her husband.

My concerns were obviously selfish and groundless, as I was not detained and was permitted to visit the Soviet Union many more times. However, I did not contact Esther or Joseph again, as shortly after my visit both were given permission to leave for Israel around 1988. I hope that their contact with me helped progress their exit permits, but I suspect that is wishful thinking on my part. Nonetheless, I am confident that my clandestine visits to them earned me a place in the KGB's filing system, as I later learnt that Esther and her family were prominent in Moscow's Jewish underground, which supported the city's *refuseniks*. Esther passed away in 2014. Her son,

Arie, also a prominent *refusenik*, now lives in Israel. Surely associating with such people should qualify me for a place in the KGB's filing system!

Miron Faynerman now lives in New Jersey while Joseph Faynerman is a successful businessman in

Fig. 15: Joseph Faynerman with his family and Esther Tukachinsky (L to R): Joseph, Vera and Frada Melamed, Nataly Faynerman, Vladimir Melamed and Esther Tukachinsky. Photo taken in the Melamed apartment in Moscow during July 1986.

Jerusalem. Both remain passionate Zionists.

The failure to locate an Australian dossier on my activities forced me to consider other possibilities, most of which I quickly rejected. While part of my work would still be covered by ASIO's 20-year open-access period, there still should be records prior to 1997. If ASIO wanted to conceal what they believed was confidential information, particularly the identity of their informants, then they could supply the file with the details of such sensitive contents redacted. To do anything different, such as withholding the whole file, would indicate that I was being treated differently from the norm. I was aware the organisation had released documents that seemed far more sensitive than anything I was involved with, so I concluded that it was highly unlikely ASIO were treating my request as a special case. Nothing seemed to make sense and I began to think that because of my robust ego I had overestimated my importance.

After considering various scenarios, I hit upon the possibility that ASIO's archivists could have filed my commercial activities with the communist countries under the heading Comalco Aluminium Limited (CAL), the public company I worked for from 1980 to 1997. CAL, which no longer exists, was a wholly-owned subsidiary of CRA Limited, a global mining company that was based in Australia. In 1996 CRA merged with the London-based RTZ to form the dual-listed company Rio Tinto. In the 1970s, well before I joined the company, Comalco had approached the Soviets to join a project to construct an alumina refinery in the Philippines. The project never eventuated, but Comalco continued to engage with the Soviets, with the aim of selling them bauxite ore from the company's mineral deposits in Cape York, Queensland.

Through the National Archives of Australia (NAA), I applied to ASIO for any files they had opened on CAL, and as result of my application I was given access to a 44-page file that had been created in November 1967 and covered the period from that date to August 1989.[6] The final date of 1989 roughly coincides with the open-access period within which ASIO's records are exempt from public access. The possibility that ASIO has additional information that it is not required to release is indicated by the title of the file: 'Comalco Aluminium Limited Volume 1', which suggests an additional, but still exempt volume.

Most of the information in the released volume relates to Comalco's discussions with Soviet trade representatives and much of this is a crude data dump, the result of ASIO's monitoring of the Soviet Embassy's Canberra telephone line. There is no analysis or discussion of any of the information obtained through the intercepts and the lack of analysis is illustrated by the phonetic spelling of names. For example, my name first appears in a transcript from the middle of January 1985, where I am recorded as 'Komisarov'; later in the month I am referred to as 'Komasarov' and in April the transcripts refer to me as 'Komisaroff'. The June intercepts record me as 'Komissarov' and 'Komasarov', while in July I am again recorded as 'Komisarov' and for the first time I am called 'Mike'. At no stage is the correct spelling – Komesaroff – used, nor is there any attempt to understand the basis of the conversations. This strongly smacks either of incompetence or of the existence of another file.

Reading 30-year-old transcripts reminded me of people I had hardly thought about, let alone had contact with, during the past two decades. On closer examination I found that the file unintentionally recorded the evolution of the Soviet Union's foreign trade representation. The early 1980s were the last of the Brezhnev years and the Soviet trade representatives were elderly, stolid non-English-speaking apparatchiks who needed to be accompanied by a translator to communicate with their Australian trade partners. Later, when Gorbachev assumed leadership of the USSR, the trade representatives were more urbane English-speaking professionals. Later again, when private companies assumed responsibility for the major part of Russia's trade representation, the people I met were cosmopolitan multilingual professionals who fronted for the oligarchs who had forcibly and corruptly taken control of Russia's heavy industries. Regrettably, there is no evidence that ASIO's agents engaged in any basic analysis of these changing characteristics of Russian trade representation and its implications for Australian trade policy.

Compared with the other files I have accessed, the CAL dossier is more heavily redacted: it has 66 pages, but 22 were totally withheld and a number of the folios that were released were extensively blacked out. With a third of the file totally withheld, the CAL dossier is also more heavily censored than the seven Komesaroff family files (total of 190 pages) all of which all have been released. Of the 44 folios in the CAL file that were released, 28 (63 per cent) are redacted, a much higher censorship rate than the seven personal files, where only 54 pages (28 per cent) contain redactions. Possibly, the CAL file could have been more stringently censored because this file involved the monitoring of a diplomatic legation and it is likely that there would have been more continuing issues of national security than there would have been in a personal file for the same historical period.

I suspect that twelve of the withheld pages in the CAL file relate to a man called Yevgeniy Zhuravlev, who was responsible for marketing Soviet metallurgical technologies. Following one heavily redacted note, an ASIO agent records that 'surveillance indicates that Zhuravlev spends some of his time out of the office playing poker machines in various clubs around Sydney'. The file note is dated 15 May 1985 and corresponds roughly with the time that Zhuravlev abruptly left Australia. At that time I had been told that he had been detained for a minor, but not political offence. I suspect, but cannot be sure, that some of the folios that were withheld relate to this incident; this action is consistent with the NAA policy of not releasing documents that contain an individual's personal details which are not relevant to Australia's security or relate to diplomats.

It is also possible that some of the withheld pages include assessments, particularly of individuals, by ASIO agents, but based on other, more complete files I have seen, analysis of raw intelligence is something that was not a feature of ASIO's work.

In addition to the CAL file, I also obtained access to two very large files on Laurence Matheson, owner of Commercial Bureau (Australia) Proprietary Limited, which represented Comalco's interests in the USSR.[7] The file says much about Matheson's own business activities, but refers only fleetingly to efforts on behalf of Comalco's marketing. Had I realised that such little effort had gone into our business, I would certainly have terminated our marketing arrangement with Matheson and his company.

Matheson was reported to be an ASIO operative who featured as a prominent *in camera* witness before the first Hope Royal Commission.[8] The NAA holds another file on Matheson which was created by ASIO, but is not available for public examination.[9]

From other NAA files and public documents I have learnt that many of the Soviet representatives I interacted with were either well connected Party members or else very senior KGB officers. I was on good terms with the ambassador, Yevgeny Samoteykin, who, immediately prior to coming to Australia in 1983, had been a personal assistant to Leonid Brezhnev (1906–82), the General Secretary of the Communist Party of the Soviet Union. I was always amused when the Ambassador affectionately referred to his previous boss, Brezhnev as the 'Old Man'. Before joining Brezhnev's team, Samoteykin had worked in the central bureau of the Soviet Ministry of Foreign Affairs, a role which, like his role with the General

Secretary, was an influential one.

John Evans – my boss at Comalco and the architect of the company's strategy for marketing bauxite to the Soviet Union – and I would regularly meet with Ambassador Samoteykin and his wife, Lara. Mrs Samoteykin was intrigued by my surname, which she believed confirmed I had a strong revolutionary heritage with ancestors who had been active in the Russian Revolution. I respected the Samoteykins too much to even attempt to dispel this illusion.

The second-ranking Soviet diplomat at the Canberra Embassy at this time was Minister Counsellor Valeri Zemskov, a charming man who spoke perfect English with only a slight accent. On one occasion John and I entertained Zemskov and his diplomatic colleagues and their families on a cruise around Sydney Harbour. My daughter, Deborah, joined us for the cruise, where she spent time chatting with Zemskov's daughter, who was a similar age. At the time none of us was aware that Zemskov was a member of the KGB's elite Special Reserve.

The KGB's Special Reserve, or Department R, was formed following the mass expulsion in 1971 of KGB officers from Great Britain and Belgium. The intention was that in the event of similar mass expulsions, there would be an in-place contingent of embassy-based KGB officers – the Special Reserve. While not engaging in any espionage activity, these officers sought to spot potential recruits, worked with front groups and performed other diplomatic functions.[10] In Zemskov's case, the press reported that one of his prime objectives was to establish contacts with Australia's Jewish community so that Moscow could cite his relationships with the community to support the claim that the Soviet Union was liberalising its system of exit visas for Soviet Jews wanting to emigrate to Israel.[11] Obviously *Gospodin* Zemskov failed in his task! He did not spot my talent, nor did he engage with me, a member of Australia's Jewish community, about the plight of Soviet Jews.

When, in 1988, the press reported his KGB connections, Zemskov dismissed the allegation with his characteristic wit and charm. He called a press conference at the embassy where he announced that, while he was flattered to have been associated with such a respected body as the KGB, he was not 'privileged' to be a member of it.[12] Despite his well-publicised denial, shortly after making that statement, Zemskov voluntarily returned to the Soviet Union, where he became an adviser to Eduard Shevardnadze, the Soviet Foreign Minister.

ASIO had been aware of Zemskov's KGB status before he came to Australia in 1986, but because of an administrative blunder, rather than being refused entry, he had been granted a diplomatic resident's visa. Despite the error, ASIO lobbied the Department of Foreign Affairs to declare Zemskov *persona non grata,* but the Department's secretary, Dr Stuart Harris, rejected these requests.[13] Because ASIO had failed to have him expelled, there can be little doubt that, during his time in Australia, Zemskov would have been closely watched by ASIO. However, despite the likelihood of ASIO's very close surveillance, I have not been able to locate any files or references that relate to Comalco's or my own contacts with Zemskov. I considered the possibility that the meetings could have been included in a file ASIO had created for John Evans, but similarly to my enquiries of ASIO regarding a file on me, the organisation report that they do not have a file on my former boss.[14]

Prior to Zemskov's arrival in Australia, the most senior KGB officer at the embassy was reported to have been Sergei Gavrilov. Gavrilov, in his role as trade representative, would, on occasion, visit me in my Melbourne office. A fairly gruff and unsophisticated individual who spoke good, though heavily accented English, Gavrilov seemed to know little about international trade and treated his embassy colleagues with contempt, characteristics that suggested that he was a member of the Soviet security services.

Gavrilov's blunt manner attracted the attention of a representative of the Department of Foreign Affairs who attended a reception at the Soviet Embassy in Canberra some time in the mid-1980s. Gavrilov encouraged the Australian official to sample some Russian vodka. After consuming the drink, the Australian noticed that the Soviet hosts were served drinks from a different bar to the one used for guests. When the Soviet barman disappeared to restock his bar, the observant Australian examined the bottles from which drinks were being poured for the Soviet hosts and found that they contained water.[15] Like

Michael Komesaroff

Fig. 16: Michael Komesaroff in Red Square outside the Kremlin, Moscow, July 1986.

the man from Foreign Affairs, I also attended many functions at the embassy, but cannot recall ever seeing any Soviet official 'under the influence'. While I did consider the possibility that my Soviet hosts could be drinking something other than hard liquor, I never had any evidence to support my suspicions.

Despite my contacts with Gavrilov and his embassy colleagues, and despite my many trips to the Soviet Union, I cannot recall any occasion where my Soviet contacts suggested, let alone hinted, that I could assist them by betraying my country or my employer by providing them with confidential information. This recollection aligns with my conclusion that the file on Comalco is unremarkable and does not suggest that any security breaches were made by me or by any of my corporate colleagues.

The absence of any files referring to my business activities in China can be explained by the fact that my first trip to China would probably not be covered by the open-access period. I also believe that, with the end of the Cold War, with two Royal Commissions on intelligence and security and with several changes in the personnel of the organisation's Director-General, ASIO is now a very different organisation from the one that it was in the 1980s.

Conclusion

This book has shown that, because of the strong support for communism among sections of the Australian Jewish community, ASIO and its predecessors took a close interest in a number of Jewish organisations and individuals, including at least seven members of the Komesaroff family. Most of these seven people were left-leaning, secular Zionistic Jews, only one of whom was known to be a member of the CPA, and he resigned from the Party because of its policies toward the creation of a Jewish State. Four of the seven Komesaroff family files were created because the subjects were associated with Jewish organisations that were being monitored. The other three files relate to one person who subscribed to the Australasian Book Society, one who was a visitor to China, and one who attended CPA lectures. The fact that there are only seven files suggests that the Komesaroff family was not targeted as such.

While the contents of the seven files differ, they do share a number of common themes. Firstly, the subjects tended to be secular Jews with an antipathy to anti-semitism and who were strong supporters of a Jewish homeland. Much of the information collected involved mundane details sourced from informants or public documents, such as electoral rolls and vehicle registration records. There is no incriminating evidence or suggestion that any of the seven people targeted were involved in any illegal activity or were a threat to Australia's security. Also, there is no evidence that any of the seven were monitored surreptitiously through telephone intercepts or other covert and intrusive surveillance methods – this suggests that they were of only peripheral interest to the counter-intelligence agencies.

Most, but not all, of the files are incomplete, and some of the missing folios appear to have been culled during the various organisational changes that culminated in the creation of ASIO. There are redactions, which were to be expected, but I believe it is extremely unlikely that the missing pages were deliberately withheld.

Each of the files includes factual errors, ranging from minor mistakes such as incorrect or out-of-date residential addresses to scandalous lapses, including confusing people with similar names and names being misspelled. In some cases, essential information such as membership of the CPA and participation in public protests seems not to have been recognised.

Overall, the files represent a collection of disparate information of varying degrees of accuracy and value, and there is no evidence of any meaningful 'big-picture' analysis from which conclusions were drawn.

These somewhat gloomy conclusions about the

Conclusion

workings of ASIO characterise an earlier Cold War period when the organisation operated with little – if any – accountability or oversight. At this time, it effectively functioned as a partisan group supporting its conservative political masters. However, following two Royal Commissions on intelligence and security which resulted in significant reforms, ASIO is now subject to greater scrutiny. The organisation now publishes an annual report that is circulated to select members of Cabinet, as well to the Leader of the Opposition. A censored version of the report is tabled in Parliament, so it is available to the wider community. Additional accountability is provided by an Inspector-General who investigates complaints about the organisation's actions, while an Appeals Tribunal has the power to review the assessments of people who receive an adverse or qualified security assessment. A Parliamentary Joint Committee on Intelligence and Security is another ingredient in ASIO's increased transparency and accountability. It is hoped that protections such as these will prevent a repeat of the characteristics of an earlier time when public resources were wasted in spying on the Komesaroff family.

Appendix

This Appendix comprises two tables that summarise the life-event statistics of first- and second-generation members of the Komesaroff family who either migrated to Australia or were born in this country. The first table provides details for the seven children of Menachem Mendel Komisaruk and his eighteen grandchildren. The second table records the details for Meir Komisaruk's descendants – his five children and eighteen grandchildren. Menachem Mendel's son, Zalman, married his first cousin Chana Reizal, Meir's daughter, so their four children are included in both tables.

Of the 44 first- and second-generation people, only thirteen second-generation descendants are alive today, with the oldest being born in 1923 and the youngest in 1947.

In each table the names are the names by which the people were known by in Australia.

Appendix

Table A1. Descendants of Menachem Mendel Komisaruk

First generation	Second generation	Country of birth	Year of birth	Year of death
Zalman Kaye*	Tessie Freedman	Russia	1909	1996
	Myer Kaye	Russia	1911	1975
	Peter Kaye	Australia	1915	1995
	Bill Kaye	Australia	1919	2012
Yaakov Leib Mendelson	Norman Mendelson	Russia	1913	1998
	Minnie Fisher	Australia	1923	1992
Yoheved Sherr	Ben Sherr	Russia	1921	2009
	Lily Chester	Australia	1923	
Bessie Rosenbaum	Max Rosenbaum	Australia	1927	2008
	Shirley Wise	Australia	1937	
	Sid Rosenbaum	Australia	1935	
Lottie Allen	Shirley Murray	Australia	1939	
Peter Komesarook	Minnie Shaul	Australia	1927	
	Ben Kaye	Australia	1929	
	Sam Komesarook	Australia	1933	1994
William Komesaroff	Beverley Harari	Australia	1939	
	Michael Komesaroff	Australia	1945	
	David Komesaroff	Australia	1947	

*Zalman Kaye was married to his first cousin, Chana Reizel Kaye, so their four children are listed twice, as descendants of both Menachem Mendel and Meir Komisaruk.

Table A2. Descendants of Meir Komisaruk

First generation	Second generation	Country of birth	Year of birth	Year of death
Chana Reizel Kaye*	Tessie Freedman	Russia	1909	1996
	Myer Kaye	Russia	1911	1975
	Peter Kaye	Australia	1915	1995
	Bill Kaye	Australia	1919	2012
Cecilia Nathan	Myer Nathan	Australia	1916	1998
	Tybel Nathan	Australia	1917	1973
	Moses Nathan	Australia	1921	1980**
Alter Komesaroff	Morris Komesaroff	Australia	1922	2007
	Tess Green	Australia	1924	
	Norman Komesaroff	Australia	1927	1965
	David Komesaroff	Australia	1933	2007
	Eddie Komesaroff	Australia	1934	
Peter Komesaroff	Thelma Webberley	Australia	1924	2015
	Miriam Mantel	Australia	1926	2017
	Judith Same	Australia	1930	
Louis Komesaroff	Max Komesaroff	Australia	1927	1988
	Tessa Silberberg	Australia	1929	1991
	Ruth Holan	Australia	1934	

* See footnote in Table A1.

** I understand that Moses (known as Mossy) died in 1980, but I have not been able to confirm the date. I have located his army service record (NAA: B883, VX78840) which reveals that during the 1940s Mossy changed his name to John Robert Spencer.

Bibliography

Books

Mark Aarons, *War Criminals Welcome: Australia a Sanctuary for Fugitive Criminals Since 1945* (Melbourne: Black Inc., 2001).

Mark Aarons, *The Family File* (Melbourne: Black Inc., 2010).

Desmond Ball and D. M. Horner, *Breaking the Codes: Australia's KGB Network, 1944-1950* (Sydney: Allen & Unwin, 1999).

Michael Berenbaum and Fred Skolnik (eds.), *Encyclopaedia Judaica, Vol. 5* (2nd ed. Detroit: Macmillan, 2007).

John Blaxland, *The Protest Years: The Official History of ASIO, 1963-1975* (Crows Nest: Allen & Unwin, 2015).

John Blaxland and Rhys Crawley, *The Secret Cold War: The Official History of ASIO, 1975-1989* (Crows Nest: Allen & Unwin, 2016).

Meredith Burgmann ed., *Dirty Secrets: Our ASIO Files* (Sydney: New South Publishing, 2014).

Frank Cain, *The Origins of Political Surveillance in Australia* (Sydney: Angus and Robertson, 1983).

Frank Cain, *The Australian Security Intelligence Organization: An Unofficial History* (Milton Park: Frank Cass, 1994).

Robert V. Daniels, *A Documentary History of Communism: Volume II, Communism and the World* (London: I. B. Taurus & Co., 1987).

Alastair Davidson, *The Communist Party of Australia: A Short History* (Stanford, California: Hoover Institution Press, 1969).

J. Doulman and D. Lee, *Every Assistance & Protection: A History of the Australian Passport* (Leichardt: Federation Press, 2008).

Theodore Draper, *American Communism and Soviet Russia* (New Jersey: Transaction Publishers, 2003).

Sofiĩa Dubnova-Ėrlikh, *The Life and Work of S. M. Dubnov: Diaspora Nationalism and Jewish History* (Indianapolis; Indiana University Press, 1990).

Chaim Freedman, *Our Father's Harvest Supplement* (privately published, 1990).

Chaim Freedman, *Eliyahu's Branches: The Descendants of the Vilna Gaon and His Family* (New Jersey: Avotaynu Inc., 1997).

Keith Freedman, *Our Father's Harvest: A History of the Komisaruk (Komesaroff) Family* (privately published, 1982).

Robert Gellately, *Stalin's Curse* (New York: Albert A. Knopf, 2013).

Nahun Gergel, *The Pogroms in the Ukraine in 1918–1921*, YIVO Annual of Jewish Social Science, vol. 6 (New York: Yiddish Scientific Institute, 1951).

Zvi Y. Gitelman, *Jewish Nationality and Soviet Politics* (New Jersey: Princeton University Press, 1972).

Elena Gover, *Russian Anzacs in Australian History* (Sydney: UNSW Press, 2005).

Emma Goldman, *My Disillusionment in Russia* (Mineola, New York: Dover Publications Inc., 2003).

Rodney Gouttman, *In Their Merit: Australian Jewry and WWI* (Melbourne: Xlibris, 2015).

David Horner, *The Spy Catchers; The Official History of ASIO, 1949–1963* (Crows Nest: Allen & Unwin, 2014).

Peter Hruby, *Dangerous Dreamers: The Australian anti-Democratic Left and Czechoslovak Agents* (Bloomington, Indiana: iUniverse, 2010).

Tony Kevin, *Return to Moscow* (Perth, Western Australia: UWA Publishing, 2017).

Lionel Kochan, *The Jews in Soviet Russia Since 1917*, 3rd ed. (Oxford: Oxford University Press, 1978).

William Komesaroff, *What the Eye Will See: An Australian Immigrant Story* (Melbourne: Makor at Lamm Jewish Library of Australia, 2014).

Jacob Leib Komesarook, *The Progress of My Migration* (privately published, 1919).

Albert S. Lindemann, *Esau's Tears: Modern Anti-Semitism and the Rise of the Jews* (Cambridge: Cambridge University Press, 2000).

David W. Lovell and Kevin Windle, *Our Unswerving Loyalty: A documentary survey of relations between the Communist Party of Australia and Moscow, 1920–1940* (Canberra: ANU E Press, 2008).

David W. Lovell, *Marx's Proletariat: The Making of a Myth* (London & New York: Routledge Library Editions, 2015).

Stuart Macintyre, *The Reds: The Communist Party of Australia from Origins to Legality* (St Leonards: Allen & Unwin, 1998).

Hilary McPhee and Tim Burstall, *The Memoirs of a Young*

Bastard: The Diaries of Tim Burstall (Melbourne: Melbourne University Press, 2012).

Peter Medding, *From Assimilation to Group Survival: A Political and Sociological Study of an Australian Jewish Community* (Melbourne: F. W. Cheshire, 1968).

Richard Overy, *Russia's War* (Middlesex: Penguin Books, 1998).

Richard Pipes, *Russia Under the Bolshevik Regime* (New York: Vintage Books, 1995).

Eric Richards, *Destination Australia: Migration to Australia Since 1901* (Sydney: UNSW Press, 2008).

Rohan Rivett, *David Rivett: Fighter for Australian Science* (privately published, 1972).

W. D. Rubinstein, *The Left, The Right and The Jews* (New York: Universe Books, 1982).

W. D. Rubinstein, *The Jews in Australia: A Thematic History Vol. II 1945 to the Present* (Port Melbourne: William Heinemann, 1991).

Victor Sebestyen, *Lenin: The Man, the Dictator, and the Master of Terror* (London: Weidenfeld and Nicholson, 2017).

Kay Saunders and Roger Daniels, *Alien Justice: Wartime Internment in Australia and North America* (St Lucia: University of Queensland Press, 2000).

Zosa Szajkowski, *Jews, Wars and Communism* (New York: Ktav Publishing, 1974).

Malcolm J. Turnbull, *Safe Haven: Records of the Jewish Experience in Australia* (Canberra: NAA, 1999).

James Waghorne and Stuart Macintyre, *Liberty: A History of Civil Liberties in Australia* (Sydney: UNSW Press, 2011).

Journal articles

Howard Adelman, 'Australia and the Birth of Israel: Midwife or Abortionist', *Australian Journal of Politics and History*, vol. 38, no. 3 (1992), pp. 354-74.

Cathy Alexander, 'What ASIO might know about you – and how to find out for sure', *Crikey*, 27 May 2014.

Frank Cain, 'Intelligence writings in Australia', *Intelligence and National Security*, vol. 6, no. 1 (1991), pp. 242-53.

Suzanne Gershowitz, 'H. V. Evatt and the Establishment of Israel: The Undercover Zionist', *The Middle East Quarterly*, vol. 13, no. 2 (2006), pp. 8-9.

Lou Jebwab, 'The Kadimah Youth Organisation in Melbourne: Reminisces, 1942–53', *Journal of the Australian Jewish Historical Society*, vol. XII part 1 (1993) pp. 179-88.

David W. Lowell, 'Unswerving Loyalty: Moscow and the Communist Party of Australia, 1920–40', *Quadrant*, May 2008, pp. 80-6.

Brendan McGeever, 'Revolution and antisemitism: the Bolsheviks in 1917', Patterns of Prejudice, vol. 51, nos. 3-4 (2017), pp. 235-52.

Philip Mendes, 'American, Australian, and other Western Jewish Communists and Soviet Anti-Semitism: Responses to the Slansky Trial and the Doctors plot 1952–1953', *American Communist History*, vol. 10, no. 2 (2011), pp. 151-68.

Philip Mendes, 'The Jewish Council to Combat Fascism and Anti-Semitism: An Historical Reappraisal', *Journal of the Australian Jewish Historical Society*, vol. X, part 6 (1989) pp. 524-41.

Philip Mendes, 'The cold war, McCarthyism, the Melbourne

Jewish Council to Combat Fascism and Anti-Semitism, and Australian Jewry 1948–1953', *Journal of Australian Studies*, vol. 24 no. 64 (2000), pp. 196-200.

Philip Mendes, 'Jews, Nazis and Communists Down Under: The Jewish Council's Controversial Campaign Against German Immigration', *Australian Historical Studies*, vol. 33 issue 119 (2002) pp. 73-92.

Bernard S. Morris, 'Communist International Front Organizations: Their Nature and Function', *World Politics*, vol. 9, no. 1 (1956), pp. 76-87.

Lawrence J. Rothberg, 'The Registration of Communist-Front Organizations: The Statutory Framework and the Constitutional Issue' *University of Pennsylvania Law Review*, vol. 113, no. 8 (1965), pp. 1270-94.

Norman Rothfield, 'Melbourne Jewry's Cold War: My Years with the Jewish Council to Combat Fascism and Anti-Semitism', *Journal of the Australian Jewish Historical Society*, vol. XI, part 6 (1993) p. 956.

Leonard Schapiro, 'The Role of Jews in the Russian Revolutionary Movement', *The Slavonic and East European Review*, vol. 40, no. 94 (1961), pp. 148-67.

Solomon M. Schwarz, 'The New Anti-Semitism of the Soviet Union', *Commentary*, June 1949, pp. 535-45.

Henry Srebrnik, 'Such Stuff as Diaspora Dreams Are Made On: Birobidzhan and the Canadian-Jewish Communist Imagination', *Canadian Jewish Studies*, vol. 10 (2002), pp. 75-107.

Elaine R. Smith, 'But What Did They Do? Contemporary Jewish Responses to Cable Street', *Jewish Culture and History*, vol. 1, no. 2 (1998), pp. 48-55.

Evan Smith, 'Against fascism, for racial equality: communists, anti-racism and the road to the Second World War in Australia, South Africa and the United States', *Labor History*, vol 58, no. 5 (2017), pp. 676-96.

Daniel C. Tabor, 'The General Awakening of Jewish Consciousness: The Development of the Jewish Students' Group in Melbourne', *Australian Jewish Historical Society Journal*, vol XXI, part 1 (2012), pp. 61-85.

Theses and dissertations

Robert Bozinovski, *The Communist Party of Australia and Proletarian Internationalism 1928–1945*, Thesis for Doctor of Philosophy, Victoria University, April 2008.

Allan C. Leibler, *The Jewish Council to Combat Fascism and Anti-Semitism*, unpublished BA (Hons) Thesis, University of Melbourne (1968).

David Rechter, *Beyond the Pale: Jewish Communism in Melbourne*, Master of Arts Thesis, University of Melbourne (1986).

Endnotes

Preface and Acknowledgements

1. Michael Komesaroff, 'Reds Under the Bed: The Security Service's Interest in My Family', *Journal of the Australian Jewish Historical Society*, vol. XXIII, part 3 (2017) pp. 418-76.
2. NAA (National Archives Australia): A9626, 241; NAA: A6119, 99; NAA: A6119, 2106.

Introduction

1. David Horner, *The Spy Catchers: The Official History of ASIO, 1949–1963* (Crows Nest: Allen & Unwin, 2014), p. 204.
2. ibid. p. 20.

Chapter 1

1. A more complete history of the Komesaroff family can be found in William Komesaroff, *What the Eye Will See: An Australian Immigrant Story* (Melbourne: Makor at Lamm Jewish Library of Australia, 2014); Keith Freedman, *Our Father's Harvest: A History of the Komisaruk*

(Komesaroff) Family (privately published, 1982); Chaim Freedman, *Our Father's Harvest Supplement* (privately published, 1990); Chaim Freedman, *Eliyahu's Branches: The Descendants of the Vilna Gaon and His Family* (New Jersey: Avotaynu Inc., 1997). The family's oral history relates that the Komisaruk surname dates to 1846 when the patriarch, Shlomo Zalman, migrated to Grafskoy, but it is possible that it predates this because in 1804 a *ukase* from Tsar Nicholas decreed that all Jews in the Russian Empire adopt family names. The 1816 Russian census for Lithuania records the name Komisaruk, the name that was used in Grafskoy.

2 In correspondence, Mel Comisarow of Canada claims the surname existed in Lithuania and he cites an 1816 Russian census of Rasseinai (180 km northwest of Vilnius) that lists the family Komisaruk. In his 1990 privately published research, *Our Father's Harvest Supplement*, Chaim Freedman raises the possibility that the name arose from the function of some members of the family as *komisars* or tax commissioners for the army supply corps.

3 Family who migrated to the United States adopted the Komisaruk transliteration.

4 Komesaroff, op. cit., p. 24.

5 'Under the Clock', *Shepparton Advertiser*, 2 August 1923, p. 5.

6 Freedman (1990), op. cit., p. 222.

7 Solomon's immigration file (National Archives of Australia (NAA): A1,1921/15433) nominates the arrival

date as 3 October, but this conflicts with contemporary newspaper reports such as the Melbourne *Argus*, 10 October 1912, p. 5, which records the date as 10 October.
8   NAA: A1, 1921/7567.
9   The Bolsheviks were the majority faction of the Russian Social Democratic Party, which was renamed the Communist Party after seizing power in the October Revolution of 1917.
10 J. Doulman and D. Lee, *Every Assistance & Protection: A History of the Australian Passport* (Leichardt: Federation Press, 2008), p. 82.
11 The *War Precautions Act* 1914 was an Act which gave the government of Australia special powers for the duration of the Great War and for six months afterwards. The powers were exercisable by regulation so they did not need to be passed by Parliament in order to become law. Some of the activities carried out under the authority of the Act included cancellation of commercial contracts with firms in enemy countries, levying of an income tax, issue of passports, price fixing, interning of 'enemy aliens' and censorship of publications and letters.
12 Stuart Macintyre, *The Reds: The Communist Party of Australia from Origins to Legality* (St Leonards: Allen & Unwin, 1998), p. 48.
13 General Jewish Labour Bund in Lithuania, Poland and Russia, known as the Bund.
14 Joseph Berger, 'Are Liberal Jewish Voters a Thing of the Past?', *New York Times*, 4 September 2014. p. PSR3.

Chapter 2

1 David Humphries, 'The spy who came in from the cold after his death', *Sydney Morning Herald*, 26 June 2010, p. 14.
2 Mark Aarons, *The Family File* (Melbourne: Black Inc., 2010), p. 154.
3 David W. Lovell and Kevin Windle, *Our Unswerving Loyalty: A documentary survey of relations between the Communist Party of Australia and Moscow, 1920–1940*, Canberra: ANU E Press, 2008), p. 40.
4 Desmond Ball and D. M. Horner, *Breaking the Codes: Australia's KGB Network, 1944–1950* (Sydney: Allen & Unwin,1999), p. 233.
5 *Royal Commission to Investigate the Facts Relating to and the Circumstances Surrounding the Communication by the Public Officials and Other Persons in Positions of Trust of Secret and Confidential Information to Agents of Foreign Power* (Ottawa: Government Printer, 1946), p. 57; National Archives of Australia (NAA): A8908, 7B. p. 65.
6 NAA: A7452, A48.
7 ibid.
8 David Horner, *The Spy Catchers: The Official History of ASIO,1949–1963* (Crows Nest: Allen & Unwin, 2014), p. 97.
9 Ball and Horner, op. cit., p. 300.
10 NAA: A456, W26/241.
11 Horner, op. cit., p. 14.
12 ibid., p. 15.

13 The second 'Red Scare' occurred immediately after World War II.
14 David W. Lowell, 'Unswerving Loyalty: Moscow and the Communist Party of Australia, 1920–40', *Quadrant*, May 2008, pp. 80-6.
15 Stuart Macintyre, *The Reds: The Communist Party of Australia from Origins to Legality* (St Leonards: Allen & Unwin, 1998), p. 41.
16 Ball and Horner, op. cit., p. 220.
17 Lowell and Windle (2008), op. cit., p. 53.
18 L. Sharkey, 'Resist the Fascist Aggressor', *Workers Weekly*, 16 September 1938, p. 1; 'Big Meetings Support Czechs', *Workers Weekly*, 30 September 1938, p. 1; 'No Bargains with Fascist Warmakers', *Workers Weekly*, 22 August 1939, p. 2.
19 'Remembering the Hebron Riots, 1929', *Forward*, 20 August 2004.
20 Myer Nathan, 'Letters to the Editor: Poland and Hitler', Melbourne *Age*, 13 January 1944, p. 2.
21 Philip Mendes, 'American, Australian, and other Western Jewish Communists and Soviet Antisemitism: Responses to the Slansky Trial and the Doctors Plot 1952–1953', *American Communist History*, vol. 10, no. 2 (2011), p. 151.
22 Frank Cain, *The Origins of Political Surveillance in Australia* (Sydney: Angus and Robertson, 1983), p. 253. Today £500 would be equivalent to $46,000.
23 Mason is a pseudonym for an Australian communist whose real identity remains unknown. It is possible that

it could refer to either Steve Purdy or Jack Miles.

24 Aarons, op. cit., p. 248.
25 Macintyre, op. cit., pp. 356-7.
26 John Blaxland, *The Protest Years: The Official History of ASIO, 1963–1975* (Crows Nest: Allen & Unwin, 2015), pp. 93-4.
27 Robert V. Daniels, *A Documentary History of Communism: Volume II, Communism and the World* (London: I. B. Taurus & Co., 1987), p. 44.
28 David McKnight, *Espionage and the Roots of the Cold War: The Conspiratorial Heritage* (Milford Park: Frank Cass, 2002), p. 61.
29 Ball and Horner, op. cit., p. 237.
30 Lara Feigel, 'Doris Lessing's MI5 file: was she a threat to the state?', *The Guardian*, 13 November 2015.
31 Blaxland, op. cit., p. 20.
32 ibid., p. 19 and p. 61.
33 David McKnight, 'Background check shows ASIO still needs to be watched', *The Sydney Morning Herald*, 8 May 2006. Under Spry, ASIO had many similarities with its adversary, the highly centralised and strongly disciplined Communist Party.
34 David McKnight, 'I pry with my little spy…', *The Sydney Morning Herald*, 31 May 2008.
35 David Horner, op. cit., p. 203.
36 NAA: A8908, 4A. pp. 127-8.
37 ibid., p. 21.
38 Horner, op. cit., p. 35.
39 Cathy Alexander, 'What ASIO might know about you – and how to find out for sure', *Crikey*, 27 May 2014.

40 Horner, op. cit., p. 204.
41 Meredith Burgmann ed., Dirty *Secrets: Our ASIO Files* (Sydney: New South Publishing, 2014), p. 35.
42 Peter Hruby, Dangerous Dreamers: The Australian anti-Democratic Left and Czechoslovak Agents (Bloomington, Indiana: iUniverse 2010), p. 150.
43 NAA: A467, SF42/103.

Chapter 3

1 National Archives of Australia (NAA): A6122, 1235.
2 ibid.
3 Royal Commission on Intelligence and Security, *Fourth Report: Volume 1,* 1978, p. 131.
4 The CPA, and other communist parties in English-speaking countries, used the term fraction to describe organisational units which were formally affiliated with, but subordinate to, the Party's district or regional branches. The term faction was not used because it implied a degree of autonomy and democracy which did not apply to the Party's centralised organisational structure which was required to adhere strictly to the Comintern's instructions.
5 Theodore Draper, *American Communism and Soviet Russia (*Piscataway, New Jersey: Transaction Publishers, 2003), p. 172.
6 Lawrence J. Rothberg, 'The Registration of Communist-Front Organizations: The Statutory Framework and the Constitutional Issue' *University of Pennsylvania Law Review*, vol. 113, no. 8 (1965), pp. 1270-94.
7 Stuart Macintyre, *The Reds: The Communist Party of*

Australia from Origins to Legality (St Leonards: Allen & Unwin, 1998), p. 257.

8   The rise and fall of the JCCFA has been well documented. For example, Philip Mendes, 'The Cold War, McCarthyism, the Melbourne Jewish Council to Combat Fascism and Anti-Semitism, and Australian Jewry 1948–1953', *Journal of Australian Studies*, vol. 24, no. 64 (2000), pp. 196-200; Philip Mendes, 'The Jewish Council to Combat Fascism and Antisemitism: An Historical Reappraisal', *Journal of the Australian Jewish Historical Society*, vol. X, part 6 (1989) pp. 524-41.

9   The JAFC was one of five similar organisations, the other four being the Women's anti-Fascist Committee, the Committee of Scientists, The All-Slavic Committee and The Youth Committee, all of which were created by the Soviet Union in early 1942 after it was invaded by Germany. These organisations were designed to attract specific Western social groups that could contribute to the Soviet Union's war effort.

10 Robert Gellately, *Stalin's Curse* (New York: Albert A. Knopf, 2013), p. 189-90.

11 ibid., pp. 348-9.

12 As pointed out later, some members of Peter's family believe that he was a member of the CPA, but there is no mention of this in his ASIO file and the available evidence suggests he was never a communist.

13 Mendes (2000), op. cit., p. 197.

14 Australia, House of Representatives 27 November 1946, Official Hansard. no. 48 (1946), p. 661.

15 H. B. Gullett, 'Admittance of Jews', Melbourne *Argus*, 12 February 1947, p. 2.

16 P. Y. Medding, *From Assimilation to Group Survival: A Political and Sociological Study of an Australian Jewish Community* (Melbourne: F. W. Cheshire, 1968), p. 154.

17 'Gullett's Jew-Baiting Raises Storm of Protests', Sydney *Tribune*, 21 February 1947, p. 4; Sydney *Tribune*, 18 March 1947, p. 5; 'Menzies Whitewashes Gullett's Jew-Baiting', Sydney *Tribune*, 11 March 1947, p. 5.

18 Australia, House of Representatives, 30 August 1945, Official Hansard. no. 35 (1945), p. 5053.

19 Howard Adelman, 'Australia and the Birth of Israel: Midwife or Abortionist', *Australian Journal of Politics and History*, vol. 38, no. 3 (1992), pp. 354-74; Suzanne Gershowitz, 'A Review of Daniel Mandel's H. V. Evatt and the Establishment of Israel: The Undercover Zionist', *Middle East Quarterly*, vol. 13, no. 2 (2006), pp. 8-9.

20 W. D. Rubinstein, *The Left, the Right and the Jews* (New York: Universe Books, 1982), p. 166.

21 V. I. Lenin, 'Critical Remarks on the National Question' in *Lenin Collected Works: Volume 20*. (Moscow: Progress Publishers, 1977), p. 50.

22 Henry Srebrnik, 'Such Stuff As Diaspora Dreams Are Made On: Birobidzhan and the Canadian-Jewish Communist Imagination', *Canadian Jewish Studies* vol. 10 (2002), p. 79.

23 Emma Goldman, *My Disillusionment in Russia* (Mineola, New York: Dover Publications Inc, 2003), p. 132.

24 In the Julian calendar then used in Russia, the date was 22 March.
25 Richard Pipes, *Russia Under the Bolshevik Regime* (New York: Vintage Books, 1995), p. 363.
26 Sofiĩa Dubnova-Ėrlikh, *The Life and Work of S. M. Dubnov, Diaspora Nationalism and Jewish History* (Indianapolis: Indiana University Press, 1990), p. 231. Steinberg was a co-founder of the Freeland League for Jewish Territorial Colonization, a body that attempted to find a refuge for persecuted European Jews. During the early years of World War II, with increasing reports of Jewish persecution, the League sought to develop an area in the Kimberley region of north-west Australia as a refuge. From 1939 to 1943, Steinberg lived in Perth, where he unsuccessfully lobbied the Federal government to support the scheme. Beverley Hooper, 'Steinberg, Isaac Nachman (1888–1957)', *Australian Dictionary of Biography* (Melbourne: Melbourne University Press, 2002), vol. 16, pp. 298-9.
27 Michael Berenbaum and Fred Skolnik (Eds.), *Encyclopedia Judaica, vol. 5 (*2nd ed. Detroit: Macmillan, 2007), pp. 91-101.
28 Tariq Ali, 'What Was Lenin Thinking?', *The New York Times*, 3 April 2017.
29 Nahum Gergel, *The Pogroms in the Ukraine in 1918–1921*, YIVO Annual of Jewish Social Science, vol. 6 (New York: Yiddish Scientific Institute, 1951), pp. 237-52; 'Ukrainians Kill Thousands of Jews', *The New York Times*, 27 May 1919, p. 2.

30. Victor Sebestyen, *Lenin: The Man, the Dictator, and the Master of Terror* (London: Weidenfeld and Nicolson, 2017), p. 447; Brendan McGeever, 'Revolution and Antisemitism: the Bolsheviks in 1917', *Patterns of Prejudice*, vol. 51, nos. 3-4 (2017), pp. 235-52.
31. Leonard Schapiro, 'The Role of Jews in the Russian Revolutionary Movement', *The Slavonic and East European Review*, vol. 40, no. 94 (1961), pp. 148-67.
32. Zvi Y. Gitelman, *Jewish Nationality and Soviet Politics* (New Jersey: Princeton University Press, 1972), p. 44.
33. The Nationalist Party of Australia became the United Australia Party and was replaced by the Australian Liberal Party in 1945. The National Party is the successor of the Country Party.
34. 'Predicts Return of Jews to Russia', *New York Times*, 25 March 1917.
35. Clara's mother, Rachel (née Namakshtansky) was a granddaughter to Pinkhas Komisaruk. In 1974 I was in Israel and Rachel told me that after decades of fruitless lobbying to have her daughter permitted to leave the Soviet Union, she wrote to the Soviet Premier, Nikita Khrushchev. In her desperation she wrote in Yiddish and shortly after posting the letter she was advised that Clara was leaving for America.
36. Evan Smith, 'Against fascism, for racial equality: communists, anti-racism and the road to the Second World War in Australia, South Africa and the United States, *Labor History*, (2017), 58:5, 676-96
37. Albert S. Lindemann, *Esau's Tears: Modern Antisemitism*

and the Rise of the Jews (Cambridge: Cambridge University Press, 2000), p. 433.
38 David W. Lovell, *Marx's Proletariat: The Making of a Myth (*London & New York*:* Routledge Library Editions, 2015), p. 227.
39 'Urgent Warning', *Jewish Chronicle*, 2 October 1936, p. 12.
40 'Mosley Received His Marching Orders', *Jewish Chronicle*, 9 October 1936, p. 7.
41 Elaine R. Smith, 'But What Did They Do? Contemporary Jewish Responses to Cable Street', *Jewish Culture and History*, vol. 1, issue 2 (1998), pp. 48-55.
42 L. Sharkey, 'Labor Movement Must Fight Antisemitism', *Workers Weekly*, 24 February 1939, p. 1; 'The Jews and International Capitalism', *Workers Weekly*, 14 March 1939, p. 3.
43 NAA: A6122, 148 Reference Copy.
44 'Moscow Note to New State Broad in Diplomatic Scope; De Jure Recognition, Wider Than That Given by United States, Indicated by Molotov – British Maintain Aloof Stand', *The New York Times*, 18 May 1948, p. 5.
45 *De jure* recognition is stronger than *de facto* recognition which is more tentative and recognises only that a government exercises control over a territory.
46 I have seen a number of secondary references that cite *The Great Soviet Encyclopaedia* of the 1930s in which Zionist migration to Palestine was said to have been lauded. The editors of the *Encyclopaedia* claimed that such migration had become a progressive factor, because

many of the immigrants were leftist workers who could be used against pro-British sheiks. Unfortunately I have not been able to access that edition of the *Encyclopaedia* to confirm this claim. I understand that the particular edition is extremely rare, because volumes of that period contained articles about people whose presence was later purged from publications during Stalin's Great Terror, so libraries tended to remove such items from public access, while many private owners disposed of their copies.

47 Mendes (2000), op. cit., p. 151.
48 Mendes (1989), op. cit., p. 525.
49 Judah Waten, 'The Professor's book is a great disappointment says fellow delegate', Sydney *Tribune*, 2 March 1960, p. 6.
50 NAA: A6122, 169.
51 ibid.
52 ibid. The feeling of insecurity coincided with a review of Russian attitudes towards its Jewish citizens which catalogued the long history of poor treatment by the Soviet Union of its Jewish inhabitants. See Solomon M. Schwarz, 'The New Antisemitism of the Soviet Union', *Commentary*, June 1949, pp. 535-45.
53 NAA: A6119, 819. The Wittner's daughter Anna married Zelman Cowen, who later became Governor General of Australia.
54 Peter Medding, *From Assimilation to Group Survival: A Political and Sociological Study of an Australian Jewish Community* (Melbourne: F. W. Cheshire, 1968), pp. 63-4.

55 David Horner, *The Spy Catchers: The Official History of ASIO, 1949–1963* (Crows Nest: Allen & Unwin, 2014), p. 253.

56 Frank Cain, 'Intelligence writings in Australia', *Intelligence and National Security,* vol. 6, no. 1 (1991), p. 249.

57 Eric Richards, *Destination Australia: Migration to Australia Since 1901* (Sydney: UNSW Press, 2008), p. 190.

58 Mark Aarons, *War Criminals Welcome: Australia a Sanctuary for Fugitive Criminals since 1945* (Melbourne: Black Inc, 2001), p. 285. Aarons also alleges that ASIO knowingly recruited Nazi war criminals and collaborators as intelligence sources and agents and used them in anti-communist operations, ibid., p. 12.

59 Philip Mendes, 'Jews, Nazis and Communists Down Under: The Jewish Council's Controversial Campaign Against German Immigration', *Australian Historical Studies*, vol. 33, no. 119 (2002), pp. 73-92.

60 Lou Jebwab, 'The Kadimah Youth Organisation in Melbourne: Reminiscences, 1942–53', *Journal of the Australian Jewish Historical Society*, vol. XII, part 1 (1993) p. 187.

61 Norman Rothfield, 'Melbourne Jewry's Cold War: My Years with the Jewish Council to Combat Fascism and Anti-Semitism', *Journal of the Australian Jewish Historical Society*, vol. XI, part 6 (1993), p. 956.

62 The NAA hold at least thirteen files on the JCCFA and several of them cover the CPA's interest in the Council. For example, NAA: A6122, 1883 – *Jewish Council to*

Combat Fascism and Antisemitism – ASIO file – Volume 7 [166 pp.]. It is likely that ASIO has more files that it has yet to release.

63 In 1945 the Jewish Board of Deputies replaced the Jewish Advisory Board as the peak Jewish community organisation in Victoria.

64 NAA: A6980, S250256.

65 Srebrnik op. cit., pp. 79-80.

66 Richard Overy, *Russia's War* (Middlesex: Penguin Books, 1998), p. 133.

67 Chimen Abramsky, 'The Biro-Bidzhan Project', in *The Jews in Soviet Russia Since 1917*, 3rd ed., Ed., Lionel Kochan (Oxford: Oxford University Press, 1978), p. 70.

68 'Birobidzhan', *The Encyclopedia and Dictionary of Zionism and Israel,* http://www.zionism-israel.com/dic/Birobidjan.htm. Gezerd was often reported on favorably by the Australian communist press, 'Anti-War Congress', *Workers' Weekly*, 14 April 1933, p. 1; 'Against Persecution of Jews', *Workers Weekly*, 3 March 1933, p. 2; 'Gezerd Meeting Refutes Anti-Jewish Tales', *Workers Weekly,* 18 January 1935, p. 6. At its peak in the 1930s, Jews represented no more than 20 per cent of Birobidzhan's population. Today the proportion is less than 5 per cent.

69 Malcolm J. Turnbull, *Safe Haven: Records of the Jewish Experience in Australia* (Canberra: NAA, 1999), p. 108; Macintyre, ibid., p. 267.

70 David Rechter, *Beyond the Pale: Jewish Communism in Melbourne,* Master of Arts Thesis, University of Melbourne (1986), pp. 38-42.

71 Jedwab, op. cit., p. 179.
72 'Social and General', *Hebrew Standard of Australasia*, 21 April 1933, p. 7; 'Religion or Politics?', *Hebrew Standard of Australasia*, 17 February 1933, p. 4.
73 'Victorian Jews Protest: Gezerd Society's Meeting', Melbourne *Age*, 11 April 1933, p. 9.
74 Turnbull, op. cit., p. 108.
75 'Kisch Case Goes to Court', Melbourne *Argus*, 13 November 1934, p. 8.
76 'Gezerd Meeting Refutes Anti-Jewish Tales', *Workers' Weekly*, 18 January 1935, p. 6. While he was born to Jewish parents, Trotsky explicitly declared his lack of interest in Jewish life or cultural kinship with Jews. He is reported to have said 'I am not a Jew but an Internationalist', Gitelman ibid., pp. 106-7.
77 NAA: A9108, Roll 4/2.
78 Today the Jewish Welfare and Relief Society is known as Jewish Care.
79 ASIO officers seemed to be avid readers of the *Australian Jewish News* and the *Australian Jewish Herald* as many of their files include clippings from these publications. ASIO regarded the Jewish *Herald* as 'absolutely loyal' while the Jewish *News* was judged to be 'definitely pro-Communist'. NAA: A6122, 444. 2 August 1943.

Chapter 4

1 National Archives of Australia (NAA): A800, S8670, records reveal that ASIO did not inherit all of its predecessor's (CIS) files.

2 NAA: A8908, 7B. pp. 78-83.
3 John Blaxland, *The Protest Years: The Official History of ASIO, 1963-1975* (Crows Nest: Allen & Unwin, 2015), p. 20.
4 NAA: A6122, 154.
5 MI5's operational security was often compromised, but its record keeping systems were judged to be of high quality.
6 'St. Kilda Maintenance Claim: Complaint About Relatives; Orders Made Against Husband', *The Prahran Telegraph*, 25 May 1928, p. 3.
7 Blaxland, op. cit., p. 20.
8 ibid., p. 243. During the Vietnam War (1962-75) I was balloted for national service but was rejected after a medical examination. I have always believed that the rejection was justified because of poor physical fitness caused by grotesque obesity; however I could have been mistaken because Blaxland reports that any person who took an active part in the anti-Vietnam or anti-conscription movement was almost certain to escape call-up because ASIO screening was designed to eliminate such people.
9 Special Branches were units within the various state police forces that cooperated with ASIO in matters of counter-intelligence.
10 Meredith Burgmann ed., *Dirty Secrets: Our ASIO Files* (Sydney: New South Wales Publishing, 2014), p. 173.
11 Aarons, op. cit., p. 241.
12 Frank Cain, *The Australian Security Intelligence*

Organization: An Unofficial History (Milton Park: Frank Cass Publishers, 1994), p. 171.

13 At his request, my uncle Yaakov Leib Mendelson was cremated and his ashes were scattered in an unmarked location.

14 *Royal Commission to Investigate the Facts Relating to and the Circumstances Surrounding the Communication by the Public Officials and Other Persons in Positions of Trust of Secret and Confidential Information to Agents of Foreign Power* (Ottawa: Government Printer, 1946), p. 57.

15 David Horner, *The Spy Catchers: The Official History of ASIO, 1949–1963* (Crows Nest: Allen & Unwin, 2014), p. 204.

16 Aarons, op. cit., p. vii.

Chapter 5

1 Within the family my uncle was known as Yaakov Leib but legally his name in Australia was Judah Leib.

2 National Archives Australia (NAA): A6126, 1331.

3 Dessau is a town 120 km south-west of Berlin in Germany.

4 Jewish Virtual Library, *Moses Mendelssohn*, http://www.jewishvirtuallibrary.org/moses-mendelssohn, accessed 1 March 2018.

5 Amos Elon, *The Pity of it All: A Portrait of Jews in Germany 1743-1933* (New York: Picador, 2002), p. 34.

6 Such fervour from CPA members was not unusual. When the Australian poet and life-long communist

Katharine Susannah Prichard died in 1969, her coffin was draped in the red communist flag.

7   David Rechter, *Beyond The Pale: Jewish Communism in Melbourne*, Master of Arts thesis, University of Melbourne (1986), p. 38.

8   ibid. p. 74. ASIO files refer to the Jewish Branch of the CPA but former Party members report there was a Jewish fraction within the Party but no specific Jewish Branch. The fraction was essentially a caucus of Jews who were members of official Party branches, for example the St Kilda Branch, but they also met as an informal group to discuss Jewish topics. The Jewish Fraction was a formal caucus in that it was recognised by the CPA's central committee.

9   J. L. Mendelson, 'Resigns from the Communist Party', *Australian Jewish News*, 1 March 1946, p. 6. A similar letter was published in the *Australian Jewish Herald* of the same date.

10 Jacob Leib Komesarook, *The Progress of My Migration* (privately published, 1919), p. 36.

11 Jacob Leib Komesarook, 'Queries and Answers', *The International Socialist*, 1 November 1919, p. 3.

12 Jacob Leib Komesarook, 'Letter of Thanks', *Ballarat Star*, 19 May 1921, p. 2.

13 The most detailed article is 'Escape from Russia: Harrowing Experiences', Grafton NSW *Daily Examiner*, 23 May 1922, p. 2; other newspaper reports include 'Conditions in Russia: Former Geelong Business Man Relates Experiences'; *Geelong Advertiser*, 5 May 1922,

p. 56; 'Brisbane Russians: Escape from the Bolsheviks', Brisbane *Daily Mail*, 4 February 1922, p. 12; 'Soviet Russia: Not Fit to Live In', *Ballarat Star*, 6 February 1922, p. 2; 'Retreat from Moscow: A Family Disillusioned – No Place Like Australia', Perth *Sunday Times*, 30 April 1922, p. 22.

14 Alexander Kerensky (1881–1970) was a moderate socialist who led the Russian Provisional government that was formed after the February Revolution of 1917. On 7 November 1917, his government was overthrown by the Bolsheviks, led by Lenin and Kerensky was forced to flee the country.

15 'The Everyday Struggle: Comrade Komesarook', Sydney *Communist*, 25 May 1922, p. 2.

16 NAA: A6126, 1331.

17 'Life in Melbourne: Party for Russian Fund', Melbourne *Argus*, 12 December 1941, p. 6.

18 'War & Working Class', Melbourne *Argus*, 6 June 1945, p. 4 and 13 June 1945, p. 9.

19 In today's money this would be equivalent to $680 which seems expensive for a subscription to a newspaper.

20 NAA: A6122, 444.

21 Robert Bozinovski points out that the CPA was also involved in the publication of various pamphlets that debunked race theories and countered racism itself, and these publications included a vast amount of literature condemning antisemitism. Robert Bozinovski, *The Communist Party of Australia and Proletarian Internationalism 1928–1945,* Thesis for Doctorate of

Philosophy, Victoria University, Melbourne, April 2008, p. 238.
22 NAA: A6122, 169.
23 NAA: A6122, 444.
24 NAA: A6122, 444. 14 October 1943.
25 Mendelson (1946), op. cit.
26 The Soviets did not pursue the policy recommended by Gaster and Piratin, and on 29 November 1947 they voted in the United Nations to partition Palestine into a Jewish and an Arab state.
27 Komesarook (1919), op. cit.
28 Zosa Szajkowski, *Jews, Wars and Communism* (New York: Ktav Publishing, 1974), p. 192.
29 J. L. Mendelson, 'Russian Revolution', Burnie *Advocate*, 17 May 1944, p. 5.
30 J. L. Mendelson, 'Hitler's Theory', *The Tribune*, 12 May 1944, p. 4.
31 NAA: B741, V/3900.
32 A mezuzah is a parchment inscribed with religious texts and attached in a case to the doorpost of a Jewish house. It is a custom to kiss the mezuzah when leaving home on a long journey.
33 Komesarook, op. cit., p. 3.

Chapter 6

1 National Archives Australia (NAA): A659,1942/1/7841
2 NAA: A6119, 6423.
3 Mrs Nathan was Cecilia Nathan (née Komisaruk), mother of Myer, Moses and Tybel.

4 Myer Nathan, 'Letters to the Editor: Poland and Hitler', Melbourne *Age*, 13 January 1944, p. 2.
5 Stuart Macintyre, *The Reds: The Communist Party of Australia from Origins to Legality* (St Leonards: Allen & Unwin, 1998), pp. 387-8.
6 Chaim Freedman, *Eliyahu's Branches: The Descendants of the Vilna Gaon and His Family* (Teaneck, New Jersey: Avotaynu Inc., 1997), p. 218. The Gaon of Vilna was a famed rabbinic scholar (1720–97) who lived in the Lithuanian town of Vilna. The Gaon believed that it was essential for a Jewish scholar to have a basic knowledge of secular subjects such as mathematics, astronomy, botany, and zoology, to be able to understand the Jewish scriptures. Freedman argues that the Komesaroff clan is descended from the Gaon of Vilna. Freedman's mother, Tessie, was Cecilia Nathan's niece and Tybel's cousin.
7 NAA: A6122, 1161; NAA: A7359, Box 14/77.
8 NAA: B883, VX78840.

Chapter 7

1 National Archives Australia (NAA): B2455, Komesaroff Peter. In his book, *In Their Merit: Australian Jewry and WWI* (Melbourne: Xlibris, 2015), p. 35, Rodney Gouttman writes that on his enlistment forms Peter declared his religion as 'Synagogue'.
2 James Waghorne and Stuart Macintyre, *Liberty: A History of Civil Liberties in Australia* (Sydney: UNSW Press, 2011), p. 67.
3 Elena Gover, *Russian Anzacs in Australian History* (Sydney: UNSW Press, 2005), p. 228.

Endnotes

4 'It Can Happen Here', *The Australian Council for Civil Liberties*, March 1944.
5 NAA: A6119, 5795.
6 David Rechter, *Beyond the Pale: Jewish Communism in Melbourne*, Master of Arts Thesis, University of Melbourne (1986), p. 57.
7 J. L. Komesaroff, 'Refugee Jews', Melbourne *Argus*, 13 June 1940, p. 8.
8 NAA: A1,1936/8862.
9 Gover, op. cit., p. 232.
10 'Jottings of Jill', *Gippsland Times*, 7 December 1942, p. 2.
11 NAA: B2455, Komesaroff Peter.
12 Today the sum of £25,000 would be equivalent to $2.0 million. 'Commodious Recreation Centres For Allied Servicemen', *Hebrew Standard of Australasia*, 7 October 1944, p. 6; 'News In Brief', Melbourne *Age*, 8 August 1941, p. 8; 'Gift to Hospital', Melbourne *Age*, 10 April 1942, p. 3. Ironically, in 1971 Peter died at the Heidelberg Hospital while being treated for the consequences of his war injuries.
13 Jacob Jona, 'Antisemitism in Australia', *Australian Jewish Herald*, 22 January 1942, p. 2.
14 J. L. Komesaroff, 'War Effort Circle's Reply', *Australian Jewish Herald*, 29 January 1942, p. 3.
15 P. Komesaroff, 'Future of Israel', Melbourne *Argus*, 17 June 1949, p. 2.
16 P. Komesaroff, 'Refugee Jews', Melbourne *Argus*, 13 June 1940, p. 8.
17 NAA: A6122, 444.

Chapter 8

1   National Archives of Australia (NAA): A6119, 6248.
2   One of the files would have involved Louis and his brother Peter while another could be that of their cousin Yaakov Leib Mendelson (formerly Komesarook). It is also possible that the fourth file could be that of Cecilia Nathan (née Komesaroff).
3   The words 'optical work' and 'blind' were used by the officer. He seems to have been unaware of the irony.
4   NAA: A6119, 6248.
5   At least seven members of the Komesaroff family in Australia enlisted in the armed forces during World War II, the oldest being my uncle, Peter Komesarook (V512320), who had come to Australia in 1922. The second generation was represented by Norman Mendelson (VX95080) and Ben Sherr (VX142376) who had both migrated to Australia as children in 1922, their Australian-born cousins Peter (VX59291) and Bill (V66167) Kaye, and Peter and Bill's cousin Morris Komesaroff (V158273) who was also born in Australia. John Spencer (VX78840), also known as Moses Nathan, the son of Cecilia Nathan (née Komisaruk) and cousin to Peter and Bill Kaye and Morris Komesaroff, was another of the second generation to enlist. Peter and Bill Kaye were the only commissioned officers in this group and Morris Komesaroff was the only member of the group to have an ASIO file. This list does not include Komesaroff spouses who also enlisted.
6   Kay Saunders and Roger Daniels, *Alien Justice: Wartime*

Endnotes

> *Internment in Australia and North America* (St Lucia: University of Queensland Press, 2000), p. 60.

7   NAA: A6122, 169.
8   At the time, *circa.* 1940, the Australian national anthem was 'G-d Save the King' and in 1937 Louis had donated a large framed photograph of the monarch, King George VI, to the Gippsland Hospital, 'Gippsland Hospital', *Gippsland Times*, 14 October 1937, p. 1.
9   NAA: A6119, 6248.
10 ibid.
11 J. L. Komesaroff, 'Jewish Council', Melbourne *Jewish News*, 19 December 1951.
12 J. L. Komesaroff, 'World Peace: Britain and Russia Hold Key', *Gippsland Times*, 20 April 1938, p. 5; J. L. Komesaroff, 'A Challenge', *Gippsland Times*, 6 July 1942, p. 1; J. L. Komesaroff, 'Correspondence: Russian Controversy', *Gippsland Times*, 14 December 1942, p. 2; J. L. Komesaroff, 'Life in Russia', *Gippsland Times*, 9 July 1942, p. 6; J. L. Komesaroff, 'The Jewish Problem', *Gippsland Times*, 10 July 1944, p. 1; J. L. Komesaroff, 'Correspondence: A Rejoinder', *Gippsland Times*, 6 July 1944, p. 1; 'Russia and the War', *Gippsland Times*, 16 November 1942, p. 4; 'The Answer – £700', *Gippsland Times,* 30 November 1942, p. 1; J. L. Komesaroff, 'All Against Hitler', Melbourne *Argus*, 1 June 1940, p. 7.
13 Louis' reported correspondence with Molotov is reminiscent of a similar letter written in 1955 by Dr H. V. Evatt, the leader of the ALP, to Molotov, seeking the Foreign Minister's confirmation that documents bought

by Vladimir and Evdokia Petrov when they defected to Australia were forgeries. 'Dr. Evatt Offers To Table Molotov's Letter', *Canberra Times*, 21 October 1955, p. 1.
14 Komesaroff (1940), op. cit., p. 7.

Chapter 9

1 National Archives Australia (NAA): A6119, 6240.
2 Anton A. Lipovak and Neonila M. Lipovak, 'Radio emissions from a group of stars in the Aquarius and Cetus constellations', *St. Petersburg Polytechnical University Journal: Physics and Mathematics*, vol 3 (2017), pp. 164-9; Torsten A. Enßlin, Sebastian Hutschenreuter, Valentina Vacca, and Niels Oppermann, 'The Galaxy in circular polarization: All-sky radio prediction, detection strategy, and the charge of the leptonic cosmic rays', *Physical Review*, vol. 96, no. 4 (2017); Jiang Xue, You Xiao-Peng, 'Research on the Relation between the Widths of Core and Cone Components of Puilsars', *Chinese Astronomy and Astrophysics,* vol. 38, no. 1 (2014).
3 'Churchmen Shout "Hitler" At Vic. Attorney-General', *Sydney Morning Herald*, 24 September 1949, p. 1.
4 £100 in 1950 would be the equivalent of $4,800 in today's money.
5 'Candid Comment', Sydney *Sunday Herald*, 2 October 1949, p. 2.
6 ibid.
7 W. D. Rubinstein, *The Jews in Australia: A Thematic*

History Vol. II 1945 to the Present (Port Melbourne: William Heinemann, 1991), p. 406.

8 Allan C. Leibler, *The Jewish Council to Combat Fascism and Anti-semitism,* unpublished BA (Hons.) Thesis, University of Melbourne (1968), p. 87.

9 *Reds in Church Deputation*, Melbourne *Herald,* 23 September 1949, p. 3.

10 NAA: A6119, 6240.

11 NAA: A467, SF42/103.

12 NAA: A6119, 6240.

13 ibid.

14 ibid.

15 NAA: A6119, 47; 'Communist Leader on CSIR Staff', *Canberra Times*, 28 March 1947, p. 1; 'Laxity in Research Screening', *Sydney Morning Herald*, 29 July 1949, p. 3; Rohan Rivett, *David Rivett: Fighter for Australian Science* (privately published, 1972), p. 10.

16 Hugo Alleyne, 'Obituary: Professor Tom Kaiser', *Independent*, 12 August 1998.

17 Daniel C. Tabor, 'The General Awakening of Jewish Consciousness: The Development of the Jewish Students' Group In Melbourne', *Australian Jewish Historical Society Journal,* vol. XXI, part 1 (2012), pp. 61-85.

18 In the early 1970s, ASIO opened a file with the title 'Jewish Study Group' (NAA; A6122, 2868), but it refers to a group organised by Melbourne-based Jewish communists, many of whom were Holocaust survivors, and which had no connection with the group established

by Dr Tabor. No members of the Komesaroff family are mentioned in this ASIO file.
19 Max Komesaroff, 'Regular Shorts', *Sydney Morning Herald*, 1 December 1987, p. 14.

Chapter 10

1 If Tessa's mother Fanny Komesaroff (née Feinberg) is included, four people in Louis Komesaroff's immediate family were the subject of ASIO files; the third sibling, Ruth Holan (née Komesaroff) is the only member of her immediate family who did not have a file.
2 National Archives of Australia (NAA): A6119, 6381.
3 Alastair Davidson, *The Communist Party of Australia: A Short History* (Stanford, California: Hoover Institution Press, 1969), p. 104.
4 Hilary McPhee and Tim Burstall, *The Memoirs of a Young Bastard: The Diaries of Tim Burstall* (Melbourne: Melbourne University Press, 2012).
5 NAA: A6119, 99.
6 ibid., 21 April 1950.
7 NAA: A6122, 130.
8 Davidson, op. cit., p. 56.

Chapter 11

1 Doug Button, 'Morris Komesaroff: A brilliant legal mind and lover of the arts', Melbourne *Herald-Sun*, 26 September 2007, p. 73.
2 'Solicitor charges QC', *Canberra Times*, 12 September 1978, p. 6.
3 National Archives of Australia (NAA): A6119, 6248.

Endnotes

4 Frank Cranston, 'ASIO Clearances: Decision by PM creates new problems', *Canberra Times*, 19 December 1972, p. 7.
5 NAA: A6119, 6248.
6 'Rift within Jewish Council', *Australian Jewish News*, 30 May 1958, p. 7.

Chapter 12

1 'Book Shop Survey', *Catalyst*, 12 March 1965, p. 3.
2 Bruce Juddery, 'Behind the door with no handle', *Canberra Times*, 6 March 1969, p. 12.
3 David McKnight, *Australian Spies and their Secrets* (St Leonards, New South Wales: Allen & Unwin 2014), p. 236.
4 Tony Kevin, *Return to Moscow* (Perth, Western Australia: UNWA Publishing, 2017), p. 65.
5 'Comalco Set to Boost Bauxite Sales to Soviets', *Sydney Morning Herald*, 13 September 1986, p. 33; Sue Neals, 'All eyes on Comalco bid for Soviet joint venture', *Australian Financial Review*, 30 May 1989; 'Letters to the Editor', *Australian Financial Review*, 6 May 1989.
6 National Archives of Australia (NAA): A6122, 2815.
7 NAA: A6119, 5321: NAA: A6119, 5322.
8 Kevin, op. cit., p. 65.
9 NAA: A5754, 1983/7007/9.
10 Jeffery T. Richelson, *A Century of Spies: Intelligence in the Twentieth Century* (New York: Oxford University Press, 1995), p. 391.
11 Norman Abjorensen, 'State of crisis in our intelligence services', *Canberra Times*, 19 April 1994, p. 7.

12 Keith Scott, 'Soviet Diplomat Denies Spying', *Canberra Times*, 19 October 1988, p. 1.
13 John Blaxland and Rhys Crawley, *The Secret Cold War: The Official History of ASIO, 1975–1989* (Crows Nest: Allen & Unwin, 2016), p. 390.
14 NAA hold a file on Zemskov that was opened by the Attorney-General, but it is not available for public access. NAA: A432, SEC1988/14532.
15 NAA: A6119, 5321.

www.ingramcontent.com/pod-product-compliance
Lightning Source LLC
Chambersburg PA
CBHW062206080426
42734CB00010B/1818